# Leave Me Alone:
# I'M JEWISH!

## My Head-On Collision with
## Jesus, Judaism and Life After Death

**Ron Cantor**

**Messiah's Mandate Publishing**
PO Box 535788
Grand Prairie, TX 75053-5788
www.MessiahsMandate.org

DESTINY IMAGE® PUBLISHERS, INC.
P.O. Box 310, Shippensburg, PA 17257-0310
"Promoting Inspired Lives."

This book and all other Destiny Image, Revival Press, MercyPlace, Fresh Bread, Destiny Image Fiction, and Treasure House books are available at Christian bookstores and distributors worldwide.

For a U.S. bookstore nearest you, call 1-800-722-6774.
For more information on foreign distributors, call 717-532-3040.
Reach us on the Internet: www.destinyimage.com.

ISBN 10: 0-7684-0374-X
ISBN 13 TP: 978-0-7684-0374-9
ISBN 13 EBook: 978-0-7684-8446-5

For Worldwide Distribution, Printed in the U.S.A.
1 2 3 4 5 6 /16 15 14 13

# DEDICATION

*To Bryan. Thank you for being persistent.*

# ACKNOWLEDGMENTS

As with my last book, *Identity Theft,* there are two people who have worked hard to make this book as mistake-free as possible, in proper English. Both Susette McLachlan and Wende Beer have sacrificed many hours editing and proofreading *Leave Me Alone — I'm Jewish.* Thank you both.

I want to thank my family, for putting up with me as I worked on this book. My office is in our living room and I work out of my apartment most of the time. Without the patience of my precious family, I could not have focused, as I needed.

The Maoz Israel office staff in the US has served me tremendously. They work hard to make sure orders are fulfilled, never complain and always encourage me. Thank you Christy, Katy, Betty and Michelle.

Also, I want to thank our shipping manager, who prefers to go unnamed. He not only gets the job done, he is one of my dearest friends.

And of course, most of all I want to thank Yeshua, My Messiah and King. My story, after all, is only a testimony of His goodness. Thank you for being patient with me, having mercy on me and never giving up on me. I love you most.

*Notes:* Most of the names, except key characters, have been changed in this book, as many of the stories are not flattering. I have done my best to accurately represent conversations, but of course, as these conversations took place over decades, they are not word for word. I believe, however, that I have preserved the integrity.

It is rare to find a perfect book, but in this day of digital books, we can correct mistakes quickly. If you find a typo in this book we would be grateful if you would drop us an email to let us know. Send it to: partners@cantorlink.com

# FOREWORD

I remember the night well. We were having a special, student-faculty dinner at a Bible college on Long Island where I served as Academic Dean. For the fun of it, the students were asked to bring in baby pictures of themselves, and we would all have to match the picture with the student. It was next to impossible! People change a lot in twenty years, especially from infancy to adulthood. But there was one picture that fooled no one: We all recognized Ron Cantor! He stood out, even as a baby. The infectious smile was there. The boundless enthusiasm was there. Even that mischievous twinkle in his eye was there. It seems like Ron was always special!

Out of the many students I have had through the years, only a few of them have become spiritual sons and daughters to me, and Ron was one of them. I love him like a son, and I am proud of him beyond words. He has been called by God to be a world-changer, and I believe, with God's help, he will fulfill his divinely appointed mission. You are about to get a glimpse into this young man's heart—a heart ablaze with love for God, love for Jesus the Messiah, and love for his Jewish people.

But don't worry about a heavy, boring read. You will enjoy every page that follows, and if you are Jewish, especially an American Jew, you will relate to many of the people, places, and events. The names may be different, but his grandparents, parents, and sister, could be your grandparents, parents, and siblings. And many of the struggles he went through will resemble the struggles of your past—or even present. I think immediately of Ron in his teen years, falling into sin and living a reckless and worthless life.

Yet even as a sinner, he was a *Jewish* sinner, and so one night, after having too much to drink at a party, it was *his mom* that he called, asking her to pick him up and bring him home. (Can you imagine this?) And he was a sinner with a sensitive conscience, stealing things as a boy, only to become guilt ridden and confess. He was a conniver too, making a way where there was no way, using his gifts, his charm, his personality to open doors that by all rights should have been closed – until God brought him to the end of himself. And then he met the Messiah!

It was the shock of Ron's life to learn that his Messiah was Jesus! In Ron's eyes, this Jesus had been the leader of an alien religion, a god worshiped by the Gentiles, a religious figure followed by the *goyim*. How could Jesus (Yeshua) be the Savior of the Jewish people and the hope of the world? Ron's life was literally turned upside down (really, right side up). And he has never been the same!

When confronted by the probing questions of Orthodox rabbis, Ron sought the God of his fathers more earnestly than ever—studying, praying, seeking *truth*. And the more he sought God and asked questions, and studied and prayed, the stronger his faith became. It is because his faith was founded on the truth!

And so Ron Cantor, together with his wonderful Israeli wife Elana and their three beautiful—and very smart!—daughters, has given his entire life to making the Messiah of Israel known, first to his own Jewish people, and then to the world. I have watched him cry out in desperate prayer, asking that God would use him to the full. I have seen him labor with zeal and perseverance, determined to overcome every obstacle and share his faith with all who will listen. And I have wept with him as we have agonized over our own kinsman after the flesh—our people Israel, our families, our childhood friends—who do not yet know the infinite love of God expressed through Yeshua our Savior and King.

Moved by divine love, Ron and Elana have given up the comforts of America and left friends and family behind to pour themselves out for Jewish men and women in the Ukraine, in Hungary, and for the past decade, Israel. And it was out of love that Ron wrote this book. May that divine love touch you and transform you, just as it has transformed Ron, just as it has transformed me, and just as it has transformed millions of others around the world who have put their trust in the living God.

I pray that as you read this book you too will come to know Ron Cantor's Lord in the same intimate and passionate way that Ron knows Him. The Messiah's yoke is easy and His burden light. Would you open your heart to Him today?

Dr. Michael L. Brown

Host, *Line of Fire* nationally syndicated radio show

Author, *Answering Jewish Objections to Jesus*, Volumes I-V

# CHAPTER ONE

## I AM ADDICTED TO...

Driving to my Hebrew class at the Jewish Community Center in Rockville, Maryland one warm April evening, I sensed the Lord say, "Son, you have been ashamed of Me in your Hebrew class."

"No, Lord! I am not ashamed of You," I protested vehemently. I knew it was silly to argue with the Almighty, but I truly didn't understand. I had always been up front and forthright about my relationship with Yeshua (Jesus). Nobody could ever have accused *me* of being embarrassed or ashamed of Him.

"Then why do you keep avoiding the subject of your faith?" I sensed Him reply.

*Ouch!* He was right. Whenever I got into conversations with my classmates, I would steer the conversation clear of religion. I guess I had become a little tired of being stereotyped as a *brainwashed-fanatic* by my Jewish friends and family. I loved my people and my culture and truly wanted them to understand why I believed in Yeshua, but the rejection had begun to wear on me.

Nevertheless, above all, I wanted to please Yeshua. I told the Lord that He was right and I was sorry, and that I wouldn't be ashamed of Him in class anymore. At that moment, I had no idea what He had in store for me that evening.

Upon my arrival at class I made a point of putting my

*Jewish Prophecy Edition New Covenant* right on top of my books for everyone to see. About midway through the class, my teacher caught sight of the Hebrew title.

"Shelcha?" she asked, which means, "Yours?"

"Ken, Sheli!" I responded, "Yes, it's mine!"

Clearly confused, she continued to teach.

Not long after that she decided to teach us a new word: *machur*, which means *addicted to* or *sold out to*. Then it came time for each student to use *machur* in a sentence.

*No way!* I thought. *I am not going to do it. You set me up, Lord! That's asking too much.* If I'd been the first person called upon to use the word in a sentence, I would definitely have chickened out, but because I was sitting in the last seat of a semi-circle there was plenty of time for me to really think about my response. In the end, I thought, *What do I have to lose? Who do I really want to please—this class or God?* Finally, it was my turn.

"Ani machur l'Yeshua!" I AM SOLD OUT TO YESHUA!

The class was stunned! They broke into a corporate uproar. 'Are you for real?' 'Is that the truth?!' Suddenly, questions started flying my way: "If Jesus is the Messiah then…?" One woman ran out to the car to get a Bible. I showed them prophecies concerning the Messiah and fielded a string of questions from the class.

Finally, a frustrated student, who had actually come to class to study Hebrew, shouted, "Can we PLEASE stop talking about religion, and get back to Hebrew?" And we did.

Now you may be wondering, "Oy vey —why in the world is a young Jewish man addicted, or sold out, to Yeshua?" For me to fully answer that, we need to go back to 1983.

## NORTH CAROLINA, 1983

*I have got to know the truth; I have got to understand; How can*

*I find out?* These were the thoughts running through my mind that dark October night in North Carolina, somewhere between Durham and Louisburg—in other words—*in the middle of nowhere.* There I was, eighteen years old, in college, and on my way back from a movie with my friend, Dean. Nothing unusual in that, except for the fact that the movie we'd just seen was about *Jesus*— and I am *Jewish!* For months, I had been longing to understand the eternal. *Just what lies beyond this life, beyond humanity?* As I was about to enter adulthood, I wanted to know if God was real, and if so, what He required of me, personally. My search was about to come to an abrupt end, as I sat in the passenger's seat of that yellow Dodge Colt with all these thoughts going through my mind.

*God, I believe You are real. I didn't believe this nine months ago but I do now. You must show me the truth. I've got to know... Is Jesus the Messiah?*

After many months of wondering, I had finally come to the conclusion that the God of Abraham was real. Yet, I could not find a relationship with God in traditional Judaism. Even fasting on Yom Kippur didn't seem to bring me any closer.

I wanted more than a religion. I wanted God—I wanted to know Him. My best friend, Bryan, had had a radical transformation in his life midway through our senior year of High School and claimed to *know* God. Even my rabbi didn't claim to *know* God—in fact, a conversation years later left me thinking He didn't *even believe in God*—yet a redhead of no consequence from Richmond, Virginia, exuded a relationship with the Almighty that I had never seen in anyone before. And he claimed it was through Jesus the Messiah! Hence my prayer, *Is Jesus the Messiah?*

Although within me there was a deep desire to know God, it was more the fear of a lost eternity that drove me to this prayer:

*I've got to know the truth!* If Heaven *was real,* then more than likely, Hell was too. Therefore, I couldn't continue to simply live my life to have fun as if there was no Day of Judgment and no one to answer to in the afterlife. Furthermore, if Heaven was real, I definitely wanted to end up there! I had to know the truth.

People spend a good portion of their lives preparing for a relatively short period of time, in the light of eternity, called *retirement.* Of course, I am not against that. However, if we are prepared to expend so much energy and forethought on our retirement, should we not invest at least as much effort in preparing ourselves for eternity? Do we not owe it to ourselves to find out:

> ... *If there is a God?*
> ... And if so, *what is He like?*
> ... *Is there a Heaven... or Hell?*
> ... And, *who goes where?*

"God, I need to kno... Aaaahhh!!" Suddenly the car began to swerve from side to side. We were out of control on a two-lane country road. *Am I going to die?* I wondered. "No, you will not die," came a confident response that arose from somewhere within me. Next, as the car continued to swerve, it began to spin around and round, and finally flipped over one and a half times, leaving us upside down in a ditch.

*"What happened next?"* you ask.

Well, clearly, I didn't die... or I wouldn't be writing this book, now would I? Before I answer, let's go back a bit further... to the sixties.

14

# CHAPTER TWO

## IN THE BEGINNING...

The year was 1965. I was born into a fast changing world. Dr. Martin Luther King led his famous march from Selma, Alabama, to Montgomery. The Vietnam War showed no signs of abating. Malcolm X was killed. The Voting Rights Act, guaranteeing voting rights to African Americans, was passed. In pop culture, Mary Poppins and the Sound of Music were released on the silver screen at the same time that the Beatles and the Rolling Stones were making rock-n-roll history.

In 1965 the average house in America cost $13,600, the average yearly income was around $6,450, gas was 31 cents a gallon and you could easily own a new car for under $3,000. And I was born into a family that fit pretty comfortably into these averages.

I was born into a lower-middle-class family in Virginia Beach, Virginia. My father, a native of Richmond, was a quiet, reserved man, while my mother, a native of Norfolk, was outgoing and vivacious. In this case opposites did attract... and they are still together! We lived in a one-story house with a few bedrooms and a den. I remember our TV was built into the wood-paneled wall in the den. These were definitely modest surroundings.

## SOL AND DOROTHY

I loved going to my grandparents' apartment on Granby Street to spend the night. They were great! Sol was as cheerful and as loving as they come. He treated his wife, Dorothy, like a queen, though many a waitress would have said she didn't deserve it, as she had very little patience with bad service and made no effort at all to hide the fact. My grandmother still retained much of the beauty she portrayed in the photographs from her youth. It was easy to see why Sol fell for her.

My sister, Michele, and I always called our grandparents by their first names. It was a habit that Michele had formed when she first began to speak. Everyone thought it was so cute that a two-year-old called her grandparents by their first names that they encouraged it. I just copied her and although my parents assumed we would eventually move on to using *Grandma* and *Grandpa*, we never did and it never felt unnatural.

Sol smoked a big smelly cigar all the time. Of course, this was before cigars were in vogue; back when most people still considered them disgusting. There was always a slobbery, half-smoked cigar, as I remember, lying around somewhere in the apartment. I also remember how he loved to tickle me until I laughed so hard my stomach hurt. As a grandfather, he was great. Dorothy was the focal point of his affections, although as earlier intimated Dorothy was *not always* the object of other people's affections. She was very opinionated and had no reservations about sharing her sentiments with others. On the other hand she was full of life and character and being with her was never boring.

From my earliest memory I knew we were Jewish and I knew that Jews were different—although I wasn't sure why. One thing, though, was clear to me—that there were a lot more of *them* (Gentiles), than of *us*. We attended Beth El Synagogue in Norfolk. Norfolk was only a hop, skip, and a jump from Virginia Beach.

Although the synagogue was a place of *Jewish identity*, it lacked the deeper dimensions of true spiritual life for me. I

16

remember as a youngster attending a religious class on the High Holy Days and being told that we do not clap in a synagogue. "It is irreverent," we were informed. Even as a child I found this a bit odd. It seemed to me that a house of worship should be full of life and vigor, not solemn and ceremonial.

## FAMILY

I thought we had a great family. My mother was (and is) beautiful. She was always there for me. Despite the fact that she was clearly more *liberal* than *conservative* politically, she always put her children before her career or finances. Even when *Casual Corner*, a local dress shop, begged her to become a manager, she routinely refused for the simple reason that she felt she needed to be home when her children arrived back from school.

My mother was not only beautiful but also affectionate and encouraging. Even when I came home from school with pitiful grades, she always told me, "Ron, you are smart, and you will do well if you apply yourself." I went through high school making D's and F's and still, I thought of myself as smart—*just because Mom said I was.* When I later graduated from college with a 3.85 GPA, I wasn't surprised. I always knew that if I applied myself, I would do well—*because Mom said so!*

(If you are not from the US, the highest GPA [Grade Point Average] is four.)

My dad was a bit different. He was quiet and mellow. Like many men of his generation, he was a good provider and a loving husband to my mother, but he was not very outgoing as a father when I was younger. Over the years he has changed, and today I consider him one of my best friends. Phil Cantor is a wonderful father *and* grandfather. He is affectionate and giving, and my children adore him.

Then there was my sister, Michele. As children, we fought nonstop. Our fighting was a constant source of stress to my parents. We fought so much that they finally quit taking us out to dinner on Sunday nights, which had been a family tradition.

## HYPERACTIVE? ME?

I take most of the blame for the fighting. I was a hyperactive child and my parents didn't know how to control me—and I had no inclination to control myself. Sitting still, even today, is very difficult for me (I've just noticed that even as I am editing this, I am standing, simply because I couldn't remain sitting any longer.). My wife has long gotten used to me leaving the table at a restaurant if the meal is taking too long to arrive. *I just need to move.* While I was growing up this trait constantly caused me to get into trouble at school and in other places where restrictions were imposed.

Not only was I frequently uncontrollable, I was filled with fears and anxieties. As a boy, I had so much fear that I did not close my eyes when I went to sleep. There were times that I would make my mother sit on the floor in her room, where I could see her from my bed, until I fell asleep.

Death was a major cause of my fears. *What happens to you when you die?* Is that it? You never exist again? The very concept of death was terrifying to me—to be gone forever. As a young child, I did not believe in God or eternal life. Before I was even six, I was convinced that when you die life is over, your body is buried, and you *cease to be* a conscious entity. It simply never dawned on me that there might be more.

I was definitely a problem child. I did not know it at the time but my mother assures me it was so. She claims I absolutely drove her nuts. I remember the day I found out that I was hyperactive.

18

When I was about eleven, I saw a book in my mother's room entitled, *Your Hyperactive Child*, and thought to myself, *I didn't know Michele was hyperactive.* Then I thought about it some more and realized—she's not! I stormed downstairs, book in hand, and screamed at my mother, "Do you think I am hyperactive? I am NOT hyperactive!"

This revelation hurt me deeply. It came as a complete shock because I'd never thought of myself in this way—different or abnormal. Yet, from that day on I viewed myself with a label. It was as if I now had a new identity—*hyperactive!*

This was fifteen years before anyone ever used the words Attention Deficit Disorder, but it was clear that I had the whole package: ADHD. I couldn't pay attention and I couldn't sit still. This made learning very difficult for me. If I may, let me just add one thing about being ADHD. While I am no doctor, it is my opinion that ADD and Hyperactivity are not *disorders,* but personalities. There was a time when children weren't required to spend seven hours a day learning, but ten hours a day on the family farm or herding cattle. No one ever had to diagnose those kids as being ADD. Not everyone, I'm convinced, was meant to *sit still.* I have learned to love who I am; who God created me to be.

All right, so it gets frustrating when I spend thirty minutes looking for my sunglasses only to realize they are on my head… or that I can get up to do one thing, do three others, sit down and realize I didn't do the thing I originally set out to do. In the end, I get it all done.

But my ADHD, if there is such a thing—might not be negative. It might be the very reason people tell me I'm a effective public speaker or the reason I have the reckless abandon to jump on an airplane to go to the middle of Nigeria. My point here is that we need to stop treating ADHD, ADD or Hyperactive children as if they have a problem. I prefer to tell them that they are different—not better, not worse, just different. Okay, now I'll climb down off my soapbox and get back to the story…

## WILLIAM AND MARGIE

My father's parents lived in Richmond, Virginia on Monument Avenue no less. Anybody even slightly familiar with Richmond knows Monument Avenue. It is one of the most beautiful stretches of real estate in America. It is a boulevard divided by a grassy tree-lined area for walking and boasts statues memorializing Virginian Confederate heroes of the Civil War like J.E.B. Stuart, Jefferson Davis, Thomas 'Stonewall' Jackson and of course Robert E. Lee, whose monument was the first to be erected in 1890.

Saying that my grandfather William, or 'Willie' as we called him, was eccentric would be an understatement. There had never been another like him. Well, except that He was very much like me, only fifty years earlier. Willie also had been a hyperactive child, and grew up to be a businessman. And if you're wanting to know what field of business he was in, it would take me less time to tell you the ones he didn't try.

He was into salvage, restaurants, multilevel marketing, and hypnotism among other things. You name it—he'd done it, or at least tried it. He was a lot of fun. I used to enjoy going out to his Lincoln (He always drove a Lincoln.) to see what kind of fun stuff he had stored in the back seat. He was such a pack rat, and his being in the salvage business always made it easy for me to find something of interest in the back seat or trunk of his Lincoln.

His most exciting venture was a restaurant that he opened in the seventies called *The Roaring Twenties*. Waiters and waitresses would perform as they worked. I didn't know it at the time,

but one of the singing waitresses, he employed, was a part-time
bank clerk named Pat Benatar, who would go on to become one
of the most famous female rock-n-roll artists in history and the
object of my desire in 1982. When she performed at the Richmond
Coliseum, I bribed my way, with *grain* alcohol, all the way to front,
wrote my number on a balloon, then pushed it in her direction.
I had no idea that all I had to do to get her number was ask my
grandfather. To tell you the truth, I don't think he even realized
that she had become famous. Anyway... she didn't call.

Willie could hypnotize people. I saw him take people back
into what we thought at the time were other lifetimes. In fact,
he once took a gentleman back so far that he had great difficulty
retrieving him. When the man finally came to himself, he was
dazed and confused for quite a while. It was really frightening.
My grandfather was truly a *one of a kind* sort of fellow, and
everyone who knew him, knew it.

My memories of my grandmother Margie are sketchy at best.
Shortly after we moved to Richmond she died of heart disease. I
was around six or seven at the time and I only remember that she
was very different from Willie. She was reserved and quiet, like
my father.

## THE SALVAGE BARN

When I was six years old my father, against his will, accepted
the position of manager at Willie's new store, The Salvage Barn. In
retrospect, we are all glad we made the move to Richmond. I don't
think any of us realized that this would be the one business of
my grandfather's that would succeed—though this was probably
largely due to my father's conservative management style. Within
a few years, Willie gave his half of the store to his children. My
father then bought out his sisters and became the co-owner and

eventually bought out his partner to become the sole owner of The Salvage Barn, Inc.

Before we moved to Richmond, we had the joy of living right on the beach for two weeks while our townhouse was being completed. One day my father's friend Martin came over with his family. The three of us went fishing. We were going to *catch dinner*. After a few hours of casting we had caught two crabs and no fish! As we were walking home feeling like our very manhood was in question (boyhood for me), we ran into two teenagers who had a bucket full of fish.

"We caught all these but we are not going to eat them. Do you guys want them?" they asked us. *Did we want them?* You'd better believe it, pal! We took the fish and proudly walked home. Back at the beach house, we boasted for hours to the ladies about our great catch, until my young conscience began to bother me. Then secretly, off to the side, I confessed the truth to my mother. Needless to say, that didn't win me any points with Martin or my dad. At six years old, my conscience was very sensitive and it bothered me that we'd lied.

We made the trek to Richmond in 1971 and moved into a small townhouse development called Three Willows Court. I quickly made new friends and one enemy. There was this boy, Bobby in the neighborhood who enjoyed picking on us. One day while I was eating a banana, Bobby began to chase me. I ran as fast as I could and loving life more than my banana, I decided to part with my snack by throwing it straight up in the air, thinking as I did, *Wouldn't it be great if he slips on the banana just like in the cartoons?* At that same moment I heard one of the most beautiful sounds my young ears had ever heard—*Bobby screaming!* I turned around just in time to see him falling to the pavement out of control, scraping his arm, with blood and everything. In general, young American Jewish boys don't tend to be blood and guts oriented and I was no different, but this was unbelievable—straight from the script. I just kept on running—no mercy.

## SCHOOL—FIRST GRADE

Soon it was time for school—first grade. I dreaded it. For the first three days I cried all the way to the classroom. My classmates heard me screaming, "But I didn't kiss my mommy good-bye," as she deposited me at Skipwith Elementary School. Try living with that for a year. One kid, who failed first grade the first time around and was a full 17% older than me, used to ask me every day "Did you kiss your mommy this morning?" That would be enough to destroy any kid's self-esteem, but I was so naïve and gullible that I actually thought he was genuinely concerned about me. It wasn't until several years later that I realized he had been mocking me.

I hated school so much that one day I went in the front door and kept walking straight out through the back door. I walked along the main road having no idea where I was going, except that I wasn't going to school! Finally, two safety patrol kids stopped me. Of course when you're six, a 12-year-old safety patrol may as well be a member of the SWAT team or Navy SEAL Team Six. They asked me where I was going. "To school," I replied.

"School is the other way."

"Not my school. My school is down the road."

"What school is that?" they asked.

It was over—I was busted.

I learned to tolerate school as I realized that for twelve more years, at least, I was stuck with it.

## GOD AND JESUS

My first encounter with the idea of Jesus came while looking through a book at school. I remember seeing a sketch of a man hanging on a cross. I went home and asked my mother about it. She explained to me that Christians believed in this man and that we, as Jews, did not. At the age of seven or eight, that was a good enough explanation for me.

Sadly, most non-religious Jews define Judaism the same way—not by what we believe or are supposed to believe, **but by what we don't believe**. That was my understanding of what a Jew was—*someone who **didn't believe** in Jesus*. I remember one morning at the bus stop all the kids began to talk about religion. That was the first time I had heard the word Catholic. We all raised our hands, identifying ourselves as either Jewish, Christian or Catholic. "What are Catholics?" I asked. The other seven and eight-year-olds explained to me with the depth and precision of a seminary student that *Catholics were also Christians, but different.* I remember being somewhat confused—but it wasn't as important an issue as playing football after school, so I didn't feel the need to pursue it.

# CHAPTER THREE

## NEW HOUSE, NEW FRIENDS

The next year we moved to a single family home at 5307 Cutshaw Avenue. Our new home was in a great location. It was within walking distance of Monument Avenue, the Jewish Community Center, Willow Lawn Shopping Center, several fast food restaurants, and two movie theaters.

Over the next five years, I learned to cuss, smoke, look at pornography and steal. Everyone on our block was Jewish except the Sotos, and they were Greek. Jewish people have lived in Richmond since the 1700's. By 1790 around one hundred Jews lived in Virginia's capital city. Around that same time the first Jewish synagogue was established: K'hal Kadosh Beth Shalom. Jewish numbers in Richmond grew steadily after Thomas Jefferson's *Virginia Statute for Religious Freedom* was passed in 1786. Influenced by a Jewish friend, Jefferson felt that Jews should have equal rights and religious freedom (which they did not have before the statute). Of course my roots in America don't go back that far. My great grandparents came from Europe to America in the early 1900's.

In our neighborhood lived the Kirschners, the Silvers, the Mandells, the Mullens, the Gilmans, the Ackmans, the Sidenbergs, the Newmans (who had a daughter, Jody, four years older than me that I was convinced was the most beautiful girl ever), the Grosses, our cousins, and many other Jewish families. My guess is that today, most of these homes are no longer owned by Jewish people. Like us, most of them eventually moved to the more affluent *West End* of Richmond.

On many summer nights the neighborhood kids would stage massive games of Hide *and Seek*. The entire neighborhood became our playground and well over twenty kids would participate. There was no fear or even thought of some of the things people worry about today—child abductions or pedophiles. Being a kid was great—we had no concept of a mortgage or car payment, of dental bills, etc. In many cases today, kids are under the same stress as their parents. I met a young teen a few years ago who was deeply worried about his parents' finances. My parents had money problems and my dad had a partner who was a daily source of stress; but *I* never knew about any of those difficulties. I was allowed to simply be a child.

As a youngster I learned early how easy it was to shoplift. I realized that you could walk into a store and take things, stick them in your pants, pockets or coat and not pay for them. If you could get out of the store without detection, they were yours. In the next several years I became a pretty good shoplifter, stealing mostly little things like candy and gum. When I turned thirteen (Ironically that is when Jewish *boys* become *men*.) I began to steal clothes, games, fishing equipment and more.

I did quite well at it, until one fateful day in the spring of 1978. David Schwartz and I were in J.C. Penney. Since we both liked to fish we decided that we needed new fishing reels. I want to say here in David's defense that he was a good Jewish boy and that it was only due to my insistence that he decided to do it. Just as we were taking the reels from their boxes and placing them in our bags, a clerk walked by and called out, "Hey, what are you doing?" We immediately started walking the other way. We should have run, but we were too scared.

Fortunately David's Uncle, Michael Goldsmith, was one of the top, if not *the* top, criminal lawyers in Richmond. Michael persuaded the county to drop the charges if we would get counseling. For the next ten weeks my parents and I attended the most torturous group counseling sessions you can imagine. These people did not understand that I was a nice Jewish kid who shoplifted every now and then—I wasn't a criminal. The other kids in the room seemed to come from truly troubled families. I hated those sessions and can't remember one productive thing that came from them. It's not that they couldn't have been productive, I just had a very bad attitude that seemed totally justified at the time.

One of the reasons I continued to find myself in hot water was my hyperactive temperament. I was constantly restless. To help control my overabundance of energy, I started taking Ritalin in during the sixth grade. The drug did help me concentrate in class, but it also made me extremely paranoid. If I sniffled, I thought the whole class was thinking about my sniffle. It completely stifled my personality. After six months my father flushed them down the toilet—and that was the end of Ritalin. Despite my being calmer, they missed *me*. It had completely changed my personality. That was thirty-five years ago and the drug has been greatly improved since then, decreasing and in some cases eliminating, many of those side effects. And in my case, I had so many internal emotional issues agitating within me, that the Ritalin simply exacerbated the inner turmoil.

# CHAPTER FOUR

## LIFE—DIVORCE AND BAR MITZVAHS

It was around this time that we moved up in the world. Just like *The Jefferson's,* a popular sitcom at the time, my father was doing very well in the retail world. Like many Jews we left the older area of Richmond and moved about fifteen minutes west of Richmond to a new development called Kingsley. Several of my parents' friends were moving there. My two best friends, Matt Gold and Kyle Shapiro, had also recently moved there.

Matt was a year older and the leader of our threesome. Kyle and I were a little intimidated by Matt. Kyle looked just like me, although he was a lot taller and everywhere we went, people thought we were brothers. His dad was just over six feet four but to us he looked like Goliath! Sadly, just as we entered high school, Kyle moved to New Jersey. His parents were divorcing and his mother wanted to leave the area and move back to her childhood home.

I will never forget the day I found out that one of my best friend's parents were planning to separate. This was new territory for me. It was Super Bowl Sunday. Kyle, Matt, and I were walking to Matt's house to watch the game. We were all sports fanatics. I could tell something was wrong. Matt was never this nice to Kyle, or me, for that matter. It seemed like everyone was acting extremely unnatural.

When we got to Matt's house, Matt privately told me that Kyle's parents were getting a divorce. "What?! What did you say?" *How could this be?* I thought. *This does not happen to us! Not to people I am close to.* I was devastated for Kyle, and I know Kyle was devastated too, even though he didn't show it that night.

## HEBREW SCHOOL

Somewhere around age seven, I began attending Beth El's Hebrew School. At first it was just Sundays, but then, as you got older, it was every Tuesday and Thursday as well, for next five years! I'd go to school five days a week and then on two of these days, I had barely put my books down before the horn would beep. *Oh, how I hated that horn!* While all my non-Jewish friends were playing football and baseball, I was in Hebrew School. I managed to make it interesting by tormenting my teachers. (Of course if I'd simply had a better attitude and a desire to learn about my heritage, it could have been a more productive and much happier experience)

Ms. Nuremberg was one of my first Hebrew School teachers. She was something else. It was in her class that I first learned about a guy in the Middle East named Arafat who liked to kill Jews. He sounded so scary; I nicknamed him *Arafatso.*

Ms. Nuremberg was a feminist and I am sure a proud supporter of the failed Equal Rights Amendment. This was during the *Women's Lib* movement of the seventies. Ms. Nuremberg was a fervent disciple. She insisted we addressed her as *Ms.*, not Miss, nor Mrs., but Ms. I would purposely call her *Mrs.* Nuremberg, and she would absolutely flip out. Several times she threw me out of the class and sent me down to Rabbi Waxman's office simply for calling her Mrs. Nuremberg. Rabbi Waxman was not much of a disciplinarian. I remember sitting in his office with a couple of other kids who'd also been kicked out of class and we just hung out with the Rabbi.... There was no punishment, no shame. Eventually they fired him.

Well, somehow I made it through Mrs. Nurem... whoops, I mean *Ms.* Nuremberg's (*Whew!*) class. I don't remember much of what I learned during those years besides... *We need to plant trees in Israel, a scary place where Arafat wants to kill Jews...*, that was about it. One thing was for sure; if you didn't go through Hebrew School you could not have a Bar Mitzvah. I did have some honor, and although I was not religious, I was committed to Judaism or at least Jewish life and culture and would become Bar Mitzvah (A son of the commandment) even if it meant enduring Hebrew School and Ms. Nuremburg.

## BECOMING A MAN—BAR MITZVAH

I celebrated my Bar Mitzvah on April 12th, 1978. I practiced for months—endless hours of memorizing words in Hebrew, learning to chant them, and working up the courage to sing in front of a thousand people. Once again, my ADHD kept me from doing all that I was supposed to do, as it was so difficult for me to set aside adequate time to prepare. This was a source of shame for me, but not sufficient enough to motivate me to buckle down.

I realized that if I didn't go through with it, I would not be able to keep the three thousand dollars in gifts that I received. I figured that singing in front of a thousand people was worth $3,000. Besides, if I didn't, Cantor Okun would have killed me. Truthfully, it was an issue of honor and fortunately, despite the inadequate preparation, I was able to pull off a fairly respectable performance.

A cantor is one who cants. Canting is the singing of the liturgy in a Jewish worship service. I often joke that I am the

Cantor who can't cant! (Although, I am not so bad...) Cantor Okun was the patriarch of Beth El and one of the toughest guys I ever met. He was the Eastern European John Wayne (Robert Deniro if you're under 40, or Jason Statham if you are in your 20's) of cantors. He must have been at least 120 years old, and had a thick Eastern European accent, but he was quick with the tongue. If you messed up your Hebrew, you were history. The great thing about Cantor Okun was that once you'd gone though your Bar Mitzvah, he became your best friend. You could almost believe he actually liked you. You had passed through to manhood—and you knew it when Cantor Okun smiled at you, because he never smiled at anyone before you were a man.

It was a grand weekend. *It was all about me!* Pictures of me were everywhere. There were photographers and presents galore, family came from all over the country and a huge party was held on Saturday night. The next morning we hosted a brunch at Richmond's Hyatt House (the most serious hotel at the time) so that all the out-of-town guests could have one more chance to *celebrate me!* It was all too short-lived to turn you into an egomaniac, and besides, you knew the following week we would all be celebrating Mike Steingold or Beth Cohen.

# CHAPTER FIVE

## WHO AM I?

Enter the teen years. The most *difficult*, I mean *exhilarating* I mean *confusing*, I mean... I mean years that bring back some very nostalgic feelings as well as a lot of pain and memories of rejection. Like many young people, I found the teen years difficult as I experienced so many emotions, peer pressure, and hormonal changes. There is so much pressure among teenagers to look good, smell good, wear the right clothes, etc. And like everyone else, I just wanted to be part of the group.

I was a slave to public opinion. I had to be popular, I had to be liked and I had to be accepted. I was a follower. I believe this stemmed from the lack of relationship with my father. Most children develop their security from a love relationship with their own father. My father and I loved each other but we did not have a deep friendship. I am so grateful that my father and I are much closer today, but that doesn't mitigate the pain I experienced as a teen.

The same year I was Bar Mitzvah'd I began drinking and smoking pot. In fact, my uncle sneaked me whiskey sours at my Bar Mitzvah. *So much for becoming a man.* I kept telling myself that I would never do anything worse than *that—that* being the current drug of choice. The truth is that I was a slave to my friends' acceptance and I would do whatever they wanted me to. Had someone brought heroin, I would have stuck a needle in my arm if that is what everyone else was doing. The first time I smoked marijuana it didn't affect me. I was told that was normal. The next time I smoked, I got high and thus I entered into my teen years relatively *stoned*.

I think the three words that best describe my teen years are *insecurity, rejection* and *rebellion*. The most important decisions I made during this time were governed by these three negative factors.

You may be wondering where God comes into this picture. I never really had much concern for God. Why be concerned about something that probably doesn't even exist? And even if there were a God, I didn't see how that affected me. My goal in life was simply to have fun at any cost.

## DRUGS AND ALCOHOL

As I said, I began drinking alcohol at thirteen. I remember one of the first times I was drunk. I was invited to a party one Friday night. The young lady's parents were out of town and she thought it would be a good idea to invite half of Richmond. One of my friends brought a pint of grain alcohol—180 proof (compared to Vodka, 80 proof). At ninety percent alcohol, it was the strongest stuff on earth. Even as stupid thirteen-year-olds, we knew you didn't drink that stuff straight. Each of us poured a little into his Seven-Up bottle. Within a very short time, I began to feel different. Everything started to buzz. I liked it.

For some reason, her parents cut their trip short and came home unexpectedly. They were furious! They found a list of everyone who was invited and called their parents.

While that encounter was *fun,* I learned very quickly that there were limits to how much you could drink and still enjoy yourself. During eighth grade, Jennifer Smith decided she would have a party (The parents, in this instance, were there to supervise.). A couple of friends and I convinced this seedy dude hanging out at a Seven-Eleven to buy us some alcohol. I was given a bottle of *Mad Dog 20/20*. It was a great value at $1.79. The nickname Mad Dog was derived from its actual name MD 20/20, the 'MD' standing for its manufacturer *Mogen David*. Yep, the same folks who make the ceremonial wine used in Jewish ceremonies like Passover and Yom Kippur, also make cheap wine for drunks.

It tasted a bit like strong grape juice. I didn't feel anything at first, so I just kept drinking until I nearly finished the bottle—and then realized that I was getting drunk—*really drunk*. I remember looking in Jennifer's bathroom mirror at myself, as if I could tell the young man in the mirror to sober up and get his act together, but it only got worse. When her parents found out that there was alcohol and thirteen-year-olds doing bad things in the basement, they stopped the party. I climbed out of a window to escape but then realized I didn't have a ride home. So I went back in and asked to use the phone and called my mother. From there, I made it to the front lawn, where I promptly sprawled out on the ground. Someone drove by and told me to get in. I had got into the car with some friends who were clearly older than I was because someone was driving, when suddenly, despite my state of mind, I remembered— "Wait, my mother is coming!" They took me back and I waited for her to arrive. When she did, I climbed into the car without a word.

Just before we got to our house my mother asked, "Ron, have you been drinking?"

I answered, "Yes." Then I said, "Ah, Mom..."

"Yes?"

"Could you please pull over?" I stuck my head out of the opened door and proceeded to throw up. I was sick. I was grounded for the next six weeks and I swore I would never drink again. And I didn't... for about a year.

At this point in my life, I had a desperate desire to be popular—to be a part of the *in* crowd. Even though I had many friends, at times I felt as though I had none. I carried a sense of rejection with me into every relationship.

## FEAR OF DEATH

I still viewed life as if it ended at death and thus, I had a horrific fear of death. I was tormented by the thought that one day I would die and cease to exist. I mentioned earlier that I felt like this as a child, but in my teen years the feeling didn't dissipate. If anything it intensified. I simply didn't see God as an option. Where was He? I didn't know one person who took God seriously.

The fact that my teen years were full of adventure and new discovery only exacerbated the fear of death. I loved life. These thoughts of death plagued my mind and would often come hard on the heels of positive thoughts. *I can't wait for camp this summer,* would be quickly followed by, *but what if you die before summer?*

My mother became concerned and took me to see Dr. Linderman, a 50-year-old, pipe-smoking, lesbian psychiatrist. She had treated me when I was younger to help me deal with the hyperactivity. She didn't help much back then and really wasn't any more of a help now. How could a woman so confused about her own identity, help me find mine? And when I challenged my mother recently in jest, "How could you have taken me to that woman?" —She simply replied "Everyone recommended her!"

Dr Linderman lived in a refurbished townhouse on Monument Avenue. It was her home/office, and there, I met her partner, if my memory serves me correctly.

Soon after I began meeting with Dr. Linderman, she asked me if I masturbated. *I didn't even know what the word meant.* When

I figured it out, I was really offended and that was the end of that. From then on I decided I would deal with my fear of death without the help of the pipe-smoking doctor who creeped me out. And I did, though these thoughts of death continued to stalk me for several more years.

## THE NEIGHBORHOOD

On Cutshaw Avenue, all the kids were Jewish—Kingsley, however, was different. Most of our neighbors were non-Jews. I made many non-Jewish friends there even though many of my Jewish friends had also moved into the neighborhood. None of these *Christian* kids, however, exhibited anything even closely resembling a relationship with God either.

All the kids in the neighborhood enjoyed Canterbury Lake. It froze over every winter. One night after a particularly healthy snowfall, several of us were at the lake. Mike Fry, a renowned bully, decided that it would be good to see if the lake was frozen. "Cantor, you're going to go first to see if the ice breaks."

I was easy to pick on because I was younger and smaller. This act of stupidity far exceeded bullying.. If I fell in, I could freeze to death or drown. But bullies rarely think of worse case scenarios. At 67 pounds in seventh grade, I was the obvious choice. As I ventured forth toward the middle of the lake, Mike and the others followed. With each step, the surface ice would break, but fortunately there was a second layer of ice that was much thicker. The first layer was from the most recent snowfall.

I slowly and carefully navigated my way toward the center. Suddenly I heard two screams and a splash. I turned around to see Mike Fry and one of the others flapping around in the freezing waters. Their arms flailed like a fish on dry ground, only they weren't fish, and they were not on land. Each time they grasped the edge of the ice to pull themselves out, the ice would break again. Finally, one of the guys who was closer to my size got down flat on the ice to help them out.

*Poetic Justice*, I thought, as images of Bobby slipping on the banana peel revisited my mind. It was a great day for *picked-on kids* everywhere

Many years later, I found a verse in the Bible that summed up that experience at the lake perfectly: "He who digs a pit will fall into it" (Proverbs 26:27).

On another occasion, Kyle and I were walking back from the frozen lake. There was snow everywhere and we began to throw snowballs at cars *(Real intelligent!)*. Suddenly this jeep came by without doors. It was the perfect target. Now the chances of me hitting that jeep were between slim and none. The chances of me hitting the guy driving were even more remote. I had a horrible arm with no power. And yet, my inner Nolan Ryan (Roger Clemons if you're 40, Stephen Strasburg if you're 20) somehow found his way out. I hummed that sucker with perfect precision and bullet-like speed. The snowball exploded on the driver's thigh. *"Aaaahhh!"* he screamed as he grabbed his leg.

*"Uh-oh!"* We began to run as fast as we could through snow-filled backyards, over fences and down alleyways. Just when we thought this guy would never find us, we came out on the other side toward the street and there he was—waiting for us. *Aaaahhh!* We turned and ran the other way in sheer terror, knowing that this guy would murder us if he caught us. We ran up to an old lady's back door, pounded on it and pleaded with her to protect us. But she appeared to be as scared of us (two screaming teens on her doorstep) as we were of our would-be executioner and refused to provide us a safe haven. Fortunately, when we turned around to courageously face what we felt sure now was certain death, he was gone.

# CHAPTER SIX

## SUMMER CAMP

I went to camp that summer for the sixth year in a row. The camp was called Timber Ridge. I loved hiking in West Virginia, biking trips, horseback riding, canoeing, and camping. Another thing I liked about camp was that I had friends there.

Fortunately the duration of camp was not a long enough for them to stop liking me. I was too young to process this reasoning fully as a teen, but such is a rejection complex. It wasn't that my friends actually stopped liking me *(What's not to like? Hello!)*, it was just that my low self-worth expected it. Plus, most of us who have struggled with rejection, cling on doubly tight when we sense a relationship is in danger—which only causes more rejection. It is a porcupine syndrome—pretty cool animal, until it wants to get close. Then you run from it.

My last year at Timber Ridge was the best. It was this year, at sixteen, that I found out I have a sense of humor and that people *really do* like me. This did much for my wounded self-esteem. I made a vow that summer that when I went back to school I would become *popular*. I would use my crazy, humorous personality to gain entrance into the coveted *in-crowd*.

## BACK TO SCHOOL

I was determined that this year would be different. During the previous year, I had developed three friendships. Bryan

McCrea, Chris Williams and Jimmy Alcott were my best friends. We did everything together until our clique began to disintegrate. Jimmy found a girlfriend, Kim Carter and Chris went his own way, but Bryan and I remained close friends. He is still one of my best friends.

An amazing thing happened when I went back to school for eleventh grade. *I actually became popular.* Now I'm not saying I became the most sought after male in the school, or the star quarterback; not even the third-string quarterback, but I broke into the ranks and developed friendships by using my crazy personality and humor. My plan had worked. My phone started to ring and people actually wanted to do things with me. I developed a whole new set of friends.

The last two years of high school seemed like an eternity. It's hard to believe that it was only a two-year period. I have so many memories from those years, most of which I'm not proud of, though every now and then when I think back, I can't keep from smiling when I think back to some of the outrageous situations in which we found ourselves (Don't tell my kids!).

And yet, there are many things I did that I wish I could undo. Like I said earlier, rebellion was a way of life for me. I thought that if I wanted something, I should get it. *It was my right.* For example, the next summer I didn't go to camp. Life was too much fun in Richmond. I did still plan on going up to Timber Ridge for their annual homecoming day, the day when they welcomed back all the former campers and counselors. I had just received my driver's license and begged my parents to let me drive to West Virginia. After hours of begging, they reluctantly consented. I woke up at 4:00 a.m. to go, but could not get the car started. When I told my parents, they said they were sorry but I could not take the Cadillac.

When I realized I had no chance of starting the Ford Fairmont Wagon, I determined that no one was going to keep me from going. I took the keys to the Cadillac and I drove off! I can still see my father running out the front door trying to stop me. I had never driven that far and having been awake since 4 a.m., I could feel my eyes beginning to shut as I cruised up I-95. Fortunately I managed to stay awake. I called my parents from Maryland where I stopped to pick up some friends.

When I got home, I received my *sentence.* For the next six months I was not allowed to drive the car. Was it worth it? *Absolutely not!* But my rebellion was not concerned with consequences. Unfortunately, that was not the last time I would do something so utterly and completely defiant.

The next year, The Who (a rock band) got back together and recorded an album and went on tour. They were coming to the Capital Center in Landover, Maryland and I planned to be there! I was dumbfounded when my mother told me that I couldn't go. I couldn't believe it. Jack Birk, David Alley, and all my other friends were allowed to go—why not me? Who did my mother think she was? She had no right to stop me from going. When my friends showed up, I brazenly and defiantly said good-bye, and walked out of the house and got in the car.

It turned out to be one of the most miserable nights of my life. Soon after we arrived at the concert, I got separated from my friends and didn't find them again until two hours after the concert! Even worse, they had the drugs! Then they almost left me behind, thinking I must have found another ride home. I spent the entire concert looking for them!

When I got home, I was in serious trouble. My parents grounded me for about four months. I was completely lying when I told my friends, "It was totally worth it—I'd do it again!"

My teachers also got to taste my bravado. My biology teacher would sometimes just tell me to go to the hall at the outset of class, so that he didn't have to go through the routine disruption of throwing me out in the middle of it. I was more than happy to oblige, as I hated biology—and never did pass it.

During my senior year, I had to write a paper for a government class. I left it until the very last minute, as usual, and then I asked my friend's mother who was involved in politics, to write it for me. She did and then I copied it into my own handwriting. I was so excited about that paper—I knew I would get an *A*. Even though I had cheated, I felt I had worked hard on it. I was totally shocked therefore, to find out I'd received an *F*; the lowest grade in the class! How could this be? I had an expert write the paper. I marched up to the teacher and said, "I want to talk about this grade!"

"We will talk after class," he replied.

"No, we will talk right now!"

"Get out of my class!"

"Gladly," I responded.

I was furious. Tyler Jones, who was on crutches, happened to be in the hall at the time. I asked to borrow one of his crutches, and I slammed it against the wall. (*Did I mention I had a temper?*)

The worst part about it was that I couldn't tell them who wrote the paper to prove it was worthy. My guess is that my teacher knew I didn't write it and that's why he failed me. I pleaded my case to Gary R. Blair, the assistant principal, but to no avail.

# CHAPTER SEVEN

## GIRLS AND FIGHTING

It was also in the eleventh grade that I met Ann Wynn. Ann was Tammy Lynch's best friend, and my friend Matt was dating Tammy. Ann was a year older than I was and I completely fell for her. The problem was, the feelings weren't entirely reciprocated. I found out that in all my relationships with females, the only ones I ever really liked for more than a few days were the ones I couldn't get. It really wasn't that I was attracted to them as much as the idea of winning them. I would be completely infatuated with a girl, until she began to like me in return, then I quickly lost interest. Ann Wynn never became completely devoted to me, therefore I remained infatuated with her. In fact, I think her sole interest in me lay in the fact that her girlfriend liked me. Once she knew she had me, *she became disinterested.* I got a taste of my own medicine.

Ann went to Hermitage High School. She and Tammy were two of the more popular girls in the school. The guys of that school were not too fond of Matt and me for obvious reasons.

One night at Mr. Gadi's, a pizza and beer joint where all the Hermitage kids hung out, Ann and I got into a big fight. I told David Fielder, who was from Hermitage and liked Ann (and hated me), that he could have her. He had a few choice words for me as well. The next thing I knew, we were all outside Mr. Gadi's ready to fight.

I was not into fighting—primarily for two reasons. First, I was fundamentally opposed to the concept of fighting over a girl (especially one who was about to dump me). Plus, if you win the fight, do you get the girl? Secondly, I was scared to death of fighting. I could never understand people who didn't mind getting hit in the face. There were two types of people whose behavior baffled me: those who were self-motivated to study and people who enjoyed getting into fistfights. I was simply not raised in a culture of fist fighting. The only fights I ever got into, were those I was at least 90 percent sure I could win.

Although I can look back on it now and laugh, at the time it was humiliating to me that I was not willing to stand up to him. The truth was that I was a coward. It was not my high principles and being willing to walk away that kept me from fighting, but pure and simple *fear*. And like every other area in my life, I searched for the easy way out. I simply wasn't tough and I despised that part of me. The funny thing is that I was a trained wrestler. Horsing around, I had thrown guys twice my size to the ground. And if I could have gotten this guy on the ground, I could have won, but I was shamefully afraid.

In the midst of all the trash talk, a fellow we'd affectionately nicknamed *Stewart the Geek,* a big guy from Hermitage, came up to us and said he wanted to fight someone. He was pretty drunk, but still he was big and intimidating. He asked me and I declined, but recommended my friend Bobby Nuckles. Bobby was a country boy, no bigger than I was, but he was deceptively tough and, unlike me, simply had no fear of fighting. Once outside a Pizza Hut, a line of people gathered and each one got to punch Bobby in the chest. He just stood there and smiled.

Bobby didn't want to fight him either, but he wasn't going to chicken out. That wasn't really an option for Bobby. He asked

Stewart's friend if he should take off his class ring and the friend laughed, "You'd better keep it on; You're going to need it!" With that, they began to fight.

Within two seconds Bobby's class ring had connected with *Stewart the Geek's* nose and blood was everywhere. In fact, I'd never seen so much blood flow from a man's nose. That stopped the fight. Mike White pulled up the car and we all jumped in and escaped. It was the big story at school Monday morning. Bobby took down *Stewart the Geek* with one blow. But it ate at me that I hadn't been willing to stand up for myself. Don't get me wrong; I think it takes a bigger man not to fight than to fight. But it is one thing to want to fight and choose to use self-control not to, and quite another to simply be scared. *I was scared.*

When Ann found out that I'd been too chicken to fight, she broke up with me for good. I am not sure whether she was upset because she'd missed her opportunity to have two boys fighting over her or simply because I hadn't been willing to fight. Either way, I was devastated. I had never experienced this feeling of heartbreak. Even though I was deeply infatuated with her and wished I'd had the courage to fight David Fielder, I still thought the idea of fighting for a girl was stupid. It took me many months, but I got over Ann.

On another occasion, I was riding the bus home when another kid from our neighborhood, Brian Black, said something to me. I can't remember what he said, but Jim Dinger made a big deal about it—like he had really insulted me. The next thing I remember, everyone wanted us to fight. *Tell me this is not happening!* I thought. *I don't want to fight.*

Each day, egged on by the other teens on the bus, Brian would taunt me. But I did not want to fight. After several days of this, and seeing that even Brian was beginning to believe *his own press,* I decided that I would have to fight him. I turned to David Duvall who was sitting next to me and said, "Don't tell anyone, but I am going to get off at Brian's stop and beat the *bleep* out of him." I didn't want anyone to know because I didn't want these idiots who had created a phony issue just to see a fight, that had caused me such turmoil all week, to have the satisfaction of watching. However, David abruptly announced to everyone on the bus, *"Ronnie's gonna fight! Ronnie's gonna fight!"*

I remembered an episode on *Happy Days*, where Fonzie, the cool guy, explained to Richie, the not-so-cool guy, that the key to winning a fight was to understand a) there are no rules and b) act crazy. It's the intimidation factor. So as soon as my feet hit the ground as I stepped off the bus, I attacked Brian from behind, throwing him to the ground. Immediately we were pulled apart. The other teens explained that I had to wait for him to be ready. That was fine with me as my adrenaline was now pumping, and I could see in Brian's eyes that he was realizing that he had made a massive miscalculation as to how this would end.

Once facing each other, I attacked again, throwing him to the ground—I was a wrestler, not a fist-fighter. I got behind him and just continued to whale on his ribs, head and ears. In a short time he gave up. Angry and embarrassed, he yelled at me, "Get off of me! I quit!" I calmly got off him, turned around and walked home. The feeling was great. The gang followed and at least for that day, I was the tough guy.

## THE DOMINION OF THE KING

The next summer, a bunch of us took jobs at King's Dominion, a local amusement park. My job was to get people to play *Whack a Mole*. It was great fun! I would use my microphone and crazy personality to draw people. Who would have thought that one day in the future, that same boy would stand before 100,000 Nigerians with a similar microphone—not inviting them to play some silly game, but to receive eternal life?

It was the most coveted game to work—and I was good at it. It was a popular gig for more than one reason. At most of the games, the worker merely gave change and the people then placed their money in the opening of a Lucite box (a type of plastic box). At the end of the day, you simply turned in the same amount of money that you started out with. All you really did was make change and hand out prizes to winners.

At *Whack a Mole* it was different. Customers paid you directly. Every now and then, when someone paid with a twenty-dollar bill, I only pretended to put it into my pouch. I would crumple it up in my hand and place it in my back pocket. After two weeks of this, I became paranoid that I would be discovered and I quit. However, I had all the beer money I would need for the rest of the summer.

## I'LL BREAK HIS LEGS!

One day at the amusement park before I quit, my friends and I met a group of girls from a summer camp. They told us where they were staying and we told them that we would stop by their hotel on our way home from work. When we arrived at the *Howard Johnson* at I-95 and Parham Road, we went up to their rooms. I have a vague memory of climbing out onto a balcony and jumping to the ground when their chaperones arrived. What happened next is not vague at all. Two large men began to run after us. We ran like the wind. We made it to our cars, jumped in, and shot out of there, just in the nick of time. It was a scene straight out of a movie.

Once we were safe, we had a good laugh. The laugh ended when I got home and my dad informed me that the manager of the Howard Johnson had called. They'd gotten our license plate numbers. He'd said that if I ever stepped foot on the grounds of his hotel again, he would break my legs. Needless to say, I've not been back since.

## SNOWBALLS

During the year I worked at Safeway grocery store. It is now Kroger's on Gaskins Road. This was back when someone would not only bag all of your groceries, but also take them to your car. Often we would take caffeine pills and work eight hours, happy as clams.

One winter day, snow had fallen. Since a bunch of my friends worked there, including Brian, Jimmy and John Harrington, we would throw snowballs at each other when returning from taking out someone's groceries. Well, John thought it would be fun to throw a snowball at me while I was taking an older lady's groceries to her car. John was very strong and from all the way across the parking lot he threw the snowball. Unfortunately instead of hitting me, it hit the woman in the face! She didn't realize that someone who worked there had thrown it, or I am sure she would have sued Safeway. The good news is that she was not hurt. Like me, John had a *Do first, think later* mentality that got him in trouble more than once.

## MY FIRST BEACH TRIP

Just before I left my job, I was able to take a week off from my *vital* work at King's Dominion to join my buddies for the first of what was to become our annual beach trip. Eight of us crowded into an old hotel room where I spent most of the next week drunk, high or both. It was there that I took LSD—acid—the first time. I quickly understood why they called it *tripping*—one hit and I was on a *trip* for the next eight hours or more. There was no turning back after taking the drug and the effects were unpredictable. The best part was that you could drink as much beer as you wanted and never get sick. However, by the time your *trip* was over you felt like your body and brain were fried, totally drained of life. It generally took my body a few days to recover.

The first time was terrifying, especially after everyone else went to sleep and I was still wired. I did not sleep at all. I could not wait for the drug to wear off. Each time I put my head down I would begin to hallucinate and think I was with my friends and that everyone was awake. Within a few seconds I would realize that it was just my imagination. Each time this happened I became even more unsettled and paranoid. When the guard drove by in a golf cart, (We were at a campground, a few miles from the beach.) I thought he was some sort of grim reaper coming to get me. After hours of panic, morning finally came and the drug wore off.

I only took the drug nine more times after that. While under its influence we felt we could actually know one another's thoughts. On another occasion I thought I could fly. I once had the feeling that if I opened up a speeding car door and jumped out, I wouldn't be hurt. Fortunately, I knew this was the drug speaking to me and that I'd have killed myself if I had actually done it.

On one *trip*, I was at a ZZ Top concert. When I began to hallucinate and think their guitars were flying forward, I began to freak-out. I told my friend Mike that we had to leave. Oddly enough, in the car on the way home I began to see a picture in my mind of Jesus and His disciples. At another concert, I kept seeing a biker dude next to me with a red bandana on his head. Each time I turned to look at him, he was not there. I walked into a bathroom once and it appeared to me that the walls were breathing! Every other drug I took—whether cocaine or simply alcohol—was for the feeling, the high. LSD was all about the experience.

My first beach trip was an excursion in rebellion and reckless living. It is a wonder that none of us was seriously hurt. One night while highly influenced by LSD, my best friend, Bryan, hitchhiked with some crazy older dude we'd met, to a bar an hour away. This fellow had sold us some drugs. His name was Mike Carpitus (His name is forever stuck in my mind though we only knew him for a few days.) and I would be very surprised if he is still alive. Once in the bar, and with no money, Bryan told us that Mike walked around the bar pouring beer from near-empty bottles into his own until it was full. Bryan finally ditched the guy and hitchhiked back to the beach. We were really worried about him. So, when he showed up around 3 a.m., we all hugged him, like a parent would embrace a child they'd lost at the mall or an amusement park. Enhanced by the drugs, we were euphoric. The first thing he asked for was a Schlitz beer!

That summer, I was either drunk, high, or both, just about every day. I could only imagine what my senior year would be like.

# CHAPTER EIGHT

## SEÑOR SENIOR

I went to school drunk on the first day. That was a first for me. Several of us had met at Freddie Ment's house for whiskey that morning. A week later I went to school high on marijuana. I thought being high at school would be really cool. I had a math test that day—the one subject in which I excelled. Pot didn't help and I failed the test. That was the first and only time I attended school high.

Even so, it wasn't long after that before I was called into Gary R. Blair's office. Both he and the other vice principal were there. *What could this be about?* I thought. I had no idea.

"Ron, we have had reports that you are coming to school on drugs. We believe it is true... even now your face is red." *I blew up!* How dare they accuse me of doing drugs! I was not on drugs (at that moment). "First of all, it is your eyes that get red, not your face, and second of all... *Bleep! Bleep! Bleepity! Bleep Bleep!!!!!*" I let them have it. The amazing thing is that I really did feel indignant even though their accusations were true. I felt that unless they could prove it, I was right—like the *innocent until proven guilty* thing.

One thing I discovered from that meeting was that I had a reputation among the teachers as being one of the worst kids in school. I hadn't realized this because, although I knew I was a jerk in school, I still believed I was a good Jewish boy. I mean, there were kids in the school far worse than I was, some who would go on to become real criminals: drug dealers, thieves, future killers, armed robbers, etc. I was brought up in a respectable home.

My guess is that most of the kids in my class would have been surprised to learn that I had this reputation with the teachers. I certainly didn't with my classmates—at least I don't think I did. I think my rebellious conduct inside the school caused the faculty to think I was far worse outside the school than I really was. They thought I was a ringleader when, in fact, I was just a desperately insecure and self-conscious kid, whose bark was far worse than his bite.

## VALIUM

Valium became the next *cool* drug to use. A small dose of Valium is relatively harmless, but multiply the normal dose several times and add alcohol... and it becomes *interesting*. Of all the drugs I took, Valium was the only drug that left me unable to remember certain things the next day. It only happened one time, but the thought of doing something wrong and not knowing about it terrified me.

On this particular night I was at a party with Eddie and Bryan. Bryan, who took quite a few of these pills, walked around the party with a beer bottle in his hand declaring, *"I am going to hit somebody with this beer bottle."* Now you have to picture this. At five foot eleven, skinny, with red hair and freckles, Bryan was not a tough looking guy. His looks, however, were deceiving. Bryan's fists were as quick as lighting and I had seen him inflict some serious pain on people who'd assumed they could easily beat him up.

One day in school Tommy Doggen was eager to get in a fight. He was picking on Jimmy. Bryan said something to him in defense of Jimmy and then Tommy was looking straight at Bryan thinking,

*Who is this punk?* He challenged Bryan to fight him. Suddenly we were all walking to the bathroom. Once inside, Tommy kept taunting Bryan, but Bryan said he wouldn't start the fight—if they were going to fight, Tommy had to start it.

Suddenly Tommy's hand was heading toward Bryan's face. The instant his hand made contact with Bryan's cheek, Bryan let loose a volley of punches, all of which landed on Tommy's face. Just then the vice-principal came in and we all ran for it.

However, on this one particular night, Bryan's normally quick response time was moving in slow motion—like sprinting in quicksand. He was drunk and on Valium and had no idea what he was saying.

He was overheard by Marshall Dodge (*And for those of you who remember Gunsmoke, yep, that was his real name!*) who then threatened to pulverize Bryan. Fortunately we stopped him. But at the hint of a fight, everyone bolted out of the house. We tried to sort things out and explain to everyone that Bryan was just high, but then somebody shoved Bryan and sent him slamming into the ground. In response, I did something very uncharacteristic for me. (It was the Valium.) I shoved the guy who I thought had shoved Bryan. Instantly people grabbed hold of both of us to keep us from fighting. Although I know it appeared to those watching that I was struggling to get free so I could fight, inside I was thinking, *Please don't let me go, please don't let me go!* And, thank God, they didn't.

On the way home I had to hold Bryan up so he could go to the bathroom. His father found him the next morning passed out halfway up the stairs. I awoke the next morning and tried with every ounce of energy to remember how the night had ended, but couldn't. The last thing I remembered was dropping Eddie off. After that—*nothing*. I was so relieved to wake up in *my own* bed and not someone else's—or in jail for that matter. We stopped taking Valium after that.

That didn't stop us, however, from continuing to do stupid things. One Friday night my friends and I walked into a redneck bar in Richmond. Soon after entering we were asked to leave. We were not really that offended, but we acted as if we were. Once we exited the establishment, I took a beer bottle and threw it as hard as I could at the windshield of the car in front of me. Only after the bottle left my hand, did I realize what an utterly stupid action that was. Amazingly, the beer bottle bounced of the windshield, causing no damage at all.

I could tell you story after story like that. It was only the mercy of God that kept my friends and me out of jail. And the worst part was that I would have been going to jail for stupidity! *What did he do? Did he steal something valuable? No, he threw a beer bottle at someone's windshield.* Not that stealing is better, but at least the thief has a motive. The vandal is just an idiot.

## TEARS

One night that continues to puzzle me to this day is the night I broke down crying in front of my friends. Up to this point you have only heard how rebellious I was. Yet, believe it or not, I was also extremely sensitive. I hurt for other people. I never enjoyed having fun at the expense of others. And more than anything, I hated for my mother to suffer because of my foolishness.

I was at Ross Miller's house with Mike White, one of my best friends, and Sheila Brewer. I called my mother and told her where I was. It was past my curfew, and she was very worried about me and let me know it. It sounded like she'd been crying. As I hung up the phone, I felt deep pain for my mom and guilty that she had been so worried. Maybe it was remorse for the endless trouble I had caused her for so many years, all welling up at once. For the next ten minutes I cried uncontrollably right in front of my three friends. I attributed it to a mixture of drugs and alcohol, as well as a genuine love for my mother. It was a strange phenomenon and something I still can't believe I did.

I guess I felt safe among friends. I thought they would understand. So I was surprised when Sheila, not the guys, ridiculed me for crying. I'd thought that of all the people there, she, being a girl, would be the most understanding. Still, I was not embarrassed that I cried. I loved my mother; and when I thought about her, in comparison to some of the people I was hanging out with, there was really no contest as to who had my affection. Despite this moment of honest concern for my mother, I continued to treat her horribly. It may be hard for you to understand how one who had such deep love for his mother could be so heartless and rebellious toward her. I wish I had an explanation.

## THE EARRING

One of my final acts of selfishness and rebellion to torment my mother was the day I came home wearing an earring. It had just become acceptable for men to wear earrings. My mother was not too excited about me being a trend-setter. I managed to hide it from her for two days. She cried when she finally saw it. Despite her pleas, I would not take it out.

The next day we were supposed to have a meeting with Assistant Principal Gary R. Blair. I don't remember the reason for the meeting, but I do remember that my mother begged me to take out my earring before the meeting. I told her I wouldn't. That night, my earring somehow got caught in my shirt as I was taking it off, and went flying across my room. I spent the next two hours looking for it but never found it. To this day, I have no idea what happened to that earring.

# CHAPTER NINE

## LEAVE ME ALONE—I'M JEWISH!

The following year would bring a significant turning point in my life. Up until this time, I had one purpose in life: *to have fun!* That was it. And since I had made my way into the cool kids' group, I was having lots of fun… still deeply insecure, and struggling with rejection—but having fun.

And then, midway through my senior year, we began to notice a change in Bryan. He was not drinking or smoking dope anymore. His attitude toward girls had changed. And then, he stopped going out with us altogether. As if we had heard he was dying of cancer, the tragic news leaked out. It was devastating. Bryan had become...

### A BORN AGAIN CHRISTIAN!

*What is a born again Christian?* I wondered. I remembered a counselor at our Jewish camp who claimed to be one. But the only difference between her and anyone else I knew, was the cross she wore around her neck. Besides, all the kids I grew up with that weren't Jewish, were supposedly Christians. Why did Bryan's life have to change so radically? Why did he have to take it so far? Couldn't he be religious and still do all the things we used to do? Again, all of our other friends claimed to be *Christians* and didn't feel the need to change their lives.

I wanted answers to these questions, so I asked Bryan. I began to understand that within Christianity there are 'cultural' Christians—people who merely go to church or call themselves *Christians*, but do not take the Bible seriously. And then there are true believers—people who profess to genuinely know God. They pattern their lives after Yeshua and believe that the Bible is God's word to mankind. They believe that Yeshua died for their sins and through His sacrifice they will have eternal life.

This made sense to me because Judaism was similar. Most of the Jewish people I knew were not religious, but very Jewish. Only a small percentage of the Jewish people I knew were deeply religious.

Apparently, Jimmy Alcott and Kim Carter (one of my best friends and his girlfriend) had become *believers* as well. *(The word 'believer' is a more accurate description than the word 'Christian', and will use that from now on. The word 'Christian' has come to apply, in a broad sense, to any person who is not Jewish, Muslim, Hindu or Buddhist.)* Jimmy talked to Bryan about his faith quite frequently. But I had no idea about Jimmy's sudden interest in Jesus, since he never talked to me about it—because I was Jewish. I didn't know he was sharing with Bryan about his faith. So, when Bryan became a believer it was a total shock. Religion was simply not part of our philosophy of fun and rebellion.

Suddenly, Jimmy and Bryan were the *dynamic duo* of religious discourse. In school we used to sit with a large group of people at lunch. For weeks after Bryan's great awakening, every day at our lunch table there was a passionate debate about religion. As a Jew, I just watched as they debated with everyone else—nominal Christians and Catholics. I was an onlooker, a spectator. Had anyone turned to me and asked me for my thoughts, I would have simply said, *'Leave me alone—I'm Jewish!'* This was between them and was fun to watch, but it had nothing to do with me.

These guys proclaimed their newly found faith to teachers, principals and students without fear. For them everyone was a prospective candidate to hear their story.

I was saddened that Bryan did not party, do drugs and get drunk with us anymore. He was my best friend and I missed him. We did get Bryan to go out with us one Saturday night. We went to *New Gate*, a bar in downtown Richmond. Across from New Gate was *Hababa's* a biker bar. I wouldn't even walk by there for fear of being harmed.

At the end of the evening, we were all getting in the car to go home: John Harrington, Greg Jones, Bryan and me. I was going to let Bryan drive because the rest of us had been drinking. However, John decided he wasn't going to sit in the back seat. We yelled and screamed at each other for a while until finally I decided I would drive. I certainly wasn't going to sit in the back seat of my own car.

The rain was pouring down and as I was turning onto I-64 at Hamilton Street I thought it might be fun to go *up* the *off* ramp! (It is amazing how I defined *fun* back then, *oy!*) I did and turned around. As I came back onto Hamilton, I lost control of the car. We spun around out of control, slamming into the curb.

The back wheel of my car twisted inward from the impact. We weren't going anywhere! We realized the police would be there soon, so Greg began tossing all the beer away from the car. (We had a couple of six-packs and we were all under age.) John, who at the time bordered on alcoholism, screamed at Greg, *"What are you doing?"*—not realizing that losing the beer was a far lesser consequence than getting arrested.

Moments later the police arrived, and we explained what happened … "This white car was coming right at us. I swerved to miss it and lost control of the car and..." The policeman bought our story and I have no idea why. However, my dad was not so gullible. Years later he told me that he knew I lied about *the white car that spun out of control*. Why that policeman didn't give me a Breathalyzer test, I'll never know. Had he done so, I would most certainly have spent the night in jail.

## FAKE IDS

You may be wondering how under-aged youths managed to obtain alcohol and gain entrance into bars. Initially, we used other people's driver's licenses, just cutting out their pictures and replacing them with our own. Most bars and convenient stores eventually caught onto this ruse as so we had to figure out another way. Actually there was one convenient store on Pouncy Tract Road that seemed willing to sell alcohol to anyone. It was quite comical. No matter how young you looked, they would sell. The problem was that they were about twenty minutes into *Hicksville* and still didn't help us get into bars. I needed something better.

And then I had an idea. I went into the DMV and pretended to be someone else—a friend of mine who was a year older. When they asked me for my ID, I told them that I had lost my license and that was why I was there. They took my picture and gave me my own ID that stated I was 18—which at the time was the legal drinking age. So with no proof of who I was, I walked out of there with a flawless fake ID.

Then they changed the law. Now you had to be twenty-one to drink alcohol. In addition, you had to show some form of proof of ID in order to get a replacement license. This meant

I had to come up with another plan, even more creative. I got Barry Glickstein, who was 21 to come down to the DMV on Broad Street with me. This was a much larger DMV than the one near my home. This was their main office and consequently there was a lot more activity. The last time I was there for my own license, I noticed that after you filled out the paperwork they told you to take a seat for twenty minutes or so before they called you to have your picture taken. So, Barry filled out all the paperwork and we took a seat. When we heard *Barry Glickstein* over the loudspeaker, I was the one who went back there and had my picture taken. I am sure if I'd been caught, I would have been in a lot of trouble. Instead, an ADHD, 17-year-old, who would barely graduate high school in a few months and looked all of fourteen, devised a plan that enabled him to walk out of a DMV with an ID that said he was twenty-one.

One time, an Alcohol and Beverage Commission officer pulled us over after I had just bought beer at a local store. My friend Jason was driving. I handed the officer my fake ID. Then, despite looking fourteen, I berated him for having nothing better to do with his time. I was so cocky. If the officer had discovered I was using a fake ID, I can't imagine what would have happened. But that was Ronnie—always looking for a laugh, without considering the consequences.

# CHAPTER TEN

## I AM NOT GOING TO HEAVEN?!

One day, not long after Bryan became a believer, he gave me a ride home from school in his mint condition 1976 blue Chevy Impala. Jimmy was also with us. They asked me if I wanted to go to a *bookstore* with them. I agreed, only to find out that it was a religious bookstore. I jokingly asked the clerk if they had any Jewish music. She showed me several albums from a group called *Lamb*. It didn't dawn on me at the time, but this was my first encounter with Jews who believed in Jesus. Joel Chernoff, the lead singer of 'Lamb' and now General Secretary of the Messianic Jewish Alliance of America, has become a good friend. I assumed they were Orthodox Jews—because everyone knows, *you can't be Jewish and believe in Jesus*—or so I was taught.

On the way home from the bookstore, the penny finally dropped and I suddenly understood what it was that Bryan believed. "You mean to tell me that if I'm not *born again*, I'm not going to HEAVEN?" I blurted out.

Bryan responded with a confident, "Yep!" His response seemed to penetrate my very being. It was as if I'd been blindfolded for seventeen years and someone had suddenly ripped the blindfold off my eyes and I could see—but, being Jewish, *I didn't like what I saw.* I had never even considered the possibility that Jesus might truly be the Messiah, nor cared.

"That's not in the Bible —not even in *your* Bible. It doesn't say anything about being *born again* in the New Testament," I declared with authority. Now this was a very interesting comment for someone who had never read the Old Covenant, much less the New Covenant, to make. But looking back, this response came from the fact that despite having been surrounded by Christians my entire life, no one had ever told me about this *being born again* business.

Bryan quickly pulled out his pocket-sized New Covenant, turned to John 3:3 and read aloud.

## YESHUA DECLARED, "I TELL YOU THE TRUTH, NO ONE CAN SEE THE KINGDOM OF GOD UNLESS HE IS BORN AGAIN."

Even though I didn't believe in the New Testament, God or Satan—the words pierced my heart like a sword. Five minutes ago, I'd been a contented agnostic—now I was being confronted with the reality of Heaven and Hell. For the first time in my life, I was facing eternity. Before that conversation, I hadn't even considered that there might be something more after death—*now I knew that there was.*

*NO!* I screamed on the inside, *This cannot be true! I am Jewish, and Jews do not believe in Jesus.*

It was one of the most devastating days of my life. I cannot tell you why or how I knew that Bryan was telling the truth, *I just did.* Yet because I was Jewish, I ran from it. Being Jewish was not my only problem with Jesus. In addition to forsaking my heritage, my people, my culture and my religion, accepting Jesus meant I would have to change my lifestyle. I loved to do bad things—pure and simple. I loved being in charge of my life. I wanted to do what I wanted to do, and when I wanted to do it. Only a few verses below from where Bryan read it continues, "This is the verdict: Light has come into the world, but men loved darkness instead of light because their deeds were evil" (John 3:19).

I saw myself in that verse. I knew it was true of me, and 'hat Yeshua, the Messiah, was real—but my love for *me* held me back.


## A SEARCH ENSUES

It was not so much a desire for Heaven as a fear of Hell that drove me to investigate further. The Bible describes Hell in precise detail. The Hebrew Scriptures speak of it as a place where "Multitudes who sleep in the dust of the earth will awake: some to everlasting life, *others to shame and everlasting contempt*" (Daniel 12:2). The New Covenant is even more explicit: "And anyone not found written in the Book of Life was cast into the lake of fire" (Revelation 20:15 NKJ). And what is the nature of the *lake of fire*? It is a 'lake of burning sulfur', where 'they will be *tormented day and night for ever and ever*' (Revelation 20:10). If there was only a minute chance that this place really existed, one would be insane not to do their best to find out more about it, to establish whether it was real or not.


## VISIONS OF HELL

Not long after this, I had a very unusual experience. I was on my way to night school. (I had to retake *Government* in order to graduate on time because of the failing grade I'd received during the first semester.) Mike White was also taking a class, so we went together. On the way to school we stopped at Cory King's house. I took one *bong-hit* (a water pipe used mainly for smoking marijuana). Normally, this wouldn't have much of an effect on me. However, by the time I got to school, I could barely drive. Once

I got into the classroom, I began to envision Hell—hundreds of people lined up and in torment, just like Bryan had told me. After an hour I grabbed Mike and said, "I gotta get out of here!" We went to a local bar and I quickly drank as much as I could. Once I was drunk, I felt much better.

I didn't want to see Bryan at all after this. I hated him. I hated who he had become. I did not want him to talk about Jesus in front of me. In fact, I made the crudest comments about Jesus just to try to get him angry. Bryan, however, remained faithful and determined. He never took offence and prayed every night for me that I would understand that Jesus was the Jewish Messiah.

Now that I was beginning to realize that God was real, and thus by implication, so were Heaven and Hell, my goal was to figure out a way to get to Heaven—without changing my lifestyle. I remember one night I was at a party, drunk, and talking to this girl named Jennifer, from my school. Her parents went to Bryan's church. So, I assumed she believed in this stuff. I told her of my dilemma—wanting to go to Heaven without changing my lifestyle. She told me, how she dealt with it.

"When I get home (from partying), I pray and ask God to forgive me." There was no attitude of remorse, no contrition, just what she thought to be an acceptable formula. Even in my zeal to create a way to Heaven on my own terms, I recognized that this was flawed theology and that she was a hypocrite. What kind of a God requires His children to ask for His forgiveness and then winks as they willfully do the same thing the following day? No, I knew this wasn't the truth. Eventually Jennifer ended up pregnant and had to get married.

## SAVE THE RECORDS

Bryan had a nice collection of record albums: Neil Young, Jimi Hendrix, Led Zeppelin, Bob Marley, etc. Word got around that Bryan planned to destroy his record collection after school that day. I was shocked! *How could he even consider doing such a thing?* And why *wasn't he ashamed of it?* He was actually boasting about it!

I felt I had a moral obligation to save these records (for myself). I left school as soon as I heard the bell. I ran out to my car and drove over to Bryan's house before he and Jimmy got there.

I walked right into Bryan's house and went upstairs. I had a familiar enough relationship with Bryan's family to be able to do this. I grabbed as many of his albums as I could and headed for the door. Too late! Bryan and Jimmy were already in the house and on their way up the stairs. I ducked my shoulder and tried to push through them. There was a struggle and I fought hard. I thought *If I can just break free, I can get to my car.* But it was no use. They prevailed… two against one. After a battle that lasted several minutes with albums flying in all directions, I surrendered.

To my chagrin, Bryan and Jimmy took several hundred albums outside and placed them on a stump. Then Bryan brought out an ax! I could not believe what I was witnessing. I knew how much Bryan treasured his collection. What had happened to him that he would do such a thing?

# CHAPTER ELEVEN

## ME? A SINNER?

I had always thought of myself as a pretty good guy. So I stole a few things here and there, and lied every now and then—*I had never killed anybody*. Then again, no one had ever shown me God's standard for good and evil… that is until Bryan shocked me when he began to show me that I was breaking God's laws regularly!

"You mean you are not allowed to sleep with anyone until you are married?!" I asked incredulously. Then he read me the seventh commandment, *You Shall Not Commit Adultery*, and explained to me that adultery included sex before marriage.

A few weeks later, I was driving home one night— or morning I should say, after having broken the seventh commandment. I'd been drunk and felt like I hadn't a care in the world. In fact, to tell you the truth, I was more focused on the stories I was going to tell my friends as the woman involved was quite a bit older than I. Although, I admit, I freaked when I heard a male enter the house—who turned out to be her *giant* son! But somehow, thankfully, I escaped undetected.

Yet as drove home I was suddenly seized with fear as I remembered Bryan's words about sex before marriage. *I knew I had sinned,* and I knew that if the Bible were true, I would be punished even for that one sin alone. Obviously that was not the first time that I'd broken one of God's commands, but it was the first time I knew it and felt guilty for it.

Before, I hadn't known what sin was and it didn't bother me; now that I knew, I was filled with guilt. Of course, that is what the Jewish rabbi, Saul of Tarsus, says in the New Covenant:

> Indeed I would not have known what sin was except through the law. For I would not have known what coveting really was if the law had not said, 'Do not covet.' But sin, seizing the opportunity afforded by the commandment, produced in me every kind of covetous desire. For apart from law, sin is dead... through the law (Torah) we become conscious of sin. (Romans 7:7-8, 3:20)

Yes, we all tend to think we are *good,* but one of the reasons God gave the Torah to Moses was to show us that no one is righteous in and of himself. The Torah testifies against us. Until that day in that car, Ron Cantor was pretty sure he was a good guy. But the Law of God came to contradict me. Is that not what Saul meant when he wrote:

> Now we know that whatever the Torah says, it says to those who are under the Torah, *so that every mouth may be silenced* and the whole world held accountable to God. (Rom. 3:19)

Yes, the Torah, specifically, the seventh commandment, silenced my self-righteousness that morning.

## GRADUATION

John Harrington and I sat behind the school listening as all of our friends graduated, while we worked on a couple of six-packs of Budweiser. It had come down to the wire for me. Although I had retaken the first semester of *Government* in night school, I'd ended up failing the second semester by *half a point*. I had a 74 and needed a 74.5 to pass. You would think the teacher would have given it to me, but no, this was her opportunity to get back at me. I can't say I blamed her—I was an extremely disrespectful student and didn't really deserve the half point. I can remember times of walking into that class and just putting my head on my desk and going to sleep.

My father appealed to the Principal, Alan Dessenberger, but he pretty much hated me. Maybe that is just the distorted view of an angry and rebellious eighteen-year-old, but the school authorities were immovable. I am sure that there was great rejoicing in the teachers' lounge that day.

Believe it or not I did end up graduating at the end of the summer with a four-year GPA of 1.7. It was a miracle that I graduated at all. I hardly ever studied, I turned my papers in late, never read and I daydreamed through most of my classes. I routinely cheated and once got a higher grade than the fellow I cheated off of. He wasn't happy! I finished high school having read one book cover to cover—*Sounder*, 98 pages. Amazingly, I have written more books since high school, than I read in high school!

I know a big part of my problem was rebellion and laziness, but a larger part of it was my ADHD. On the other hand, without my ADHD, I wouldn't be me. It is part of my story and part of who I am.

Most people really don't know what it's like to not be able to sit still and focus. Even when I wanted to do well, it was difficult to concentrate. I would have been a much better student if I'd not had to grapple with my hyperactivity. The truth is, I couldn't even comprehend what it would be like to be one of those students who looked forward to learning—someone who was motivated to study. I simply had no desire to learn.

There was one person in the school system who did understand me. Unfortunately, I cannot remember his name. He was a guidance counselor. When I was in the seventh grade at Byrd Middle School, he recommended to the principal that I move on to the eighth grade even though I'd failed seventh. He was one of the few people, other than my mother, who truly believed in me. The school went along with his recommendation, and I was moved up.

The fact that this man believed in me and thought that I was smart, meant the world to me. Never underestimate the power of encouragement. My mother always told me that I was smart. Even when I brought home horrible grades, she would still say, "You are smart. If you ever applied yourself you would do well." This guidance counselor was the same. He believed I could do well. It was because of them that despite horrible grades, I never felt stupid. And they were right. Even though I graduated with a 1.7 GPA, only a few years later, I would graduate Bible School near the top of my class with a 3.85 GPA.

## BACK TO THE BEACH

That summer, my buddies and I (and the rest of Richmond's youth) took our annual trip to the beach. My friend Eddie Simmons and I were sitting on the bed in our hotel one afternoon, when we started talking about Bryan and Jimmy and their faith. Eddie confessed that he believed it was real. I told him that I thought it might be as well. Then I said something radical. "Maybe we should become believers!" There was a pause... Eddie thought about it for a minute and then said, "Nah, I don't want to do that." And that was that.

Eddie had become my best friend in Bryan's absence and twenty plus years later we are still in contact. He even invited me last year to perform the ceremony at his wedding. Sadly, I could not be in Florida at that time. We even planned to attend college together at Louisburg Junior College in North Carolina. At the last minute, however, Eddie informed me that he had changed his mind and wasn't going to go to college.

## LOUISBURG JUNIOR COLLEGE

My idea of college was *just another party* but without a curfew, parents or rules. I quickly made friends at college and every night we were out drinking at Louisburg's one and only bar.

At the end of September I decided to take LSD one last time. I only took half of a hit. My friend Joey and I were up all night. Around the middle of the night, those of us who were on LSD got into a very intense conversation about religion. They were very surprised to find out that their Jewish friend was so interested in Jesus.

The next morning, Joey and I were *fried*. We went to the cafeteria, had breakfast and began to talk about our lives. I cannot remember ever being as depressed as I was that morning. We looked at our lives and knew we were losers. We were in college simply to have fun. My life was going nowhere. I felt like I had let my mother down. As I said, she always told me that I was smart, but there I was—wasted on LSD and wasting my parents' money on tuition. Yet, by noon, I was feeling much better and by evening I was drinking again.

## MODERN DAY JUDAISM

I knew that if I was going to consider taking religion

seriously, I needed to begin with Judaism. Despite the fact that all of the original followers of Jesus were Jewish, and found no contradiction in believing that He was the Messiah and remaining Jewish (How could finding the *Jewish* Messiah make you un-Jewish?), I'd been taught that the two were incompatible—irreconcilable. Thus, I mistakenly thought that embracing Yeshua would mean leaving Judaism. And I wasn't completely mistaken, in that such a decision would have sent shock waves not only through my family but also through much of the Jewish community in Richmond. While I may have known that I was still Jewish—I would not be treated as if I was.

So, why embrace the shame associated with a Jew believing in Jesus, if I could find the same thing in traditional Judaism? Why cause my family such embarrassment if there was hope of connecting with God without Jesus? As Yom Kippur (the Jewish Day of Atonement) approached, I was determined to fast for the first time. Jews believe that fasting on Yom Kippur will cause God to forgive all our sins for that year.[1] I wanted to make a sincere effort to be righteous during the fast. My commitment would be tested. That evening a bizarre thing happened. Jennifer, the girl who claimed to be a believer but made little effort to live like one, approached me and made it abundantly clear what her desires were. She basically threw herself at me. To her surprise (and mine!), I turned her down. I had never done such a thing, as opportunities like that for a young man without values or proper respect for women, didn't come around every weekend. But that night it would not—it could not—happen. If there was a God, I was going to find Him. Not even a pretty young girl throwing herself at me was going to derail my search.

1　　　　Here is an article I wrote that show the true meaning of fasting: http://roncan.net/PKYQ5b

As the fast ended, I felt no closer to God than before. I felt no sense of forgiveness or assurance that He was even listening. I *was* hungry, though.

## MY MOST IMPORTANT QUESTION

I went back to school and really did not think much about it for a month or so. In the middle of October, I came back to Richmond for fall break. Louisburg gave us three days off in the fall, so with the weekend, I had a five-day vacation. On Friday I saw Bryan. We were sitting in his blue Impala when, once again, the conversation turned to religion.

"Bryan, is your life really better now that you are a believer?"

This question had to be asked. I loved to party and live life crazily, and I knew that at one time Bryan did as well. I had to know how living for Yeshua compared to the fun life that I was presently living. I thought I knew what his answer would be. He would say, "Well, Ron, my life is boring and dull. I don't have fun anymore, but at least I know I am going to Heaven." That was my concept of what it meant to be a believer—you live a boring life for about eighty years and your reward for sacrificing all your fun is that you get to go to Heaven. If this were true, it still seemed like a pretty good trade off—considering that eternity is *forever* and this life is a mere vapor in comparison. But Bryan did not respond as I thought.

*"My life is awesome! I know God!"* Bryan exclaimed with a face full of light and life. I had never seen someone so full of joy. When he said, *"I know God!"* I knew he was telling the truth. He confessed that he missed the old life at times but he made it clear that having a personal relationship with Jesus was a million times better in comparison.

I could not believe this. All my life I'd been looking for fun, for the next high—the next great thrill or story to tell on Monday. Now, here was Bryan telling me that the ultimate high is in God. I'd gone to synagogue all my life and frankly I thought it was boring. When I was younger, I remember always seeing the rabbi's son working hard around the Hebrew School. I was told he was training to be a rabbi like his dad. (Though in the end, I think he went into law.) I would wonder to myself *Why in the world Rabbi Berman's son would want to be a rabbi? What a boring career.* Of course, my idea of religion was simply tradition. I never considered the possibility of *knowing God, seeing miracles or actually feeling His presence.* Until Bryan, I'd never heard anyone refer to God as Someone I could actually know—Someone with Whom I could have a real relationship.

It stands to reason that no matter how amazing a life I could make for myself, God's perfect plan for me would be better. Until this, I didn't see God as Someone Who would fill me with joy and send me around the world to do His work. I still thought of God as cold, distant and boring. Yet the God I saw in the face of an exuberant Bryan was anything but boring.

"Okay Bryan, I will go with you to your congregation on Sunday."

I was intrigued. I had to meet these people who thought they knew God. Sunday morning came, and the phone rang. It was early and I was a little hung over from the night before. Whatever determination I had had on the Friday to go with Bryan to his congregation completely evaporated before the prospect of simply going back to sleep. I hung up the phone. If Bryan had waited this long, he could surely wait until the next time I was in Richmond.

Bryan may have been willing to wait, *but God was not.* The next week would be the most mind-blowing week of my life.

# CHAPTER TWELVE

## STAIRWAY TO HEAVEN

Nothing could have prepared me for what happened next. I got a ride back to Louisburg that afternoon from a girl who also lived in Richmond. I got to my room and opened the door. No one had been in my room for five days and the door was locked. As soon as I walked in, my turntable (Big CD Player for you younger folks) began to play the song *Stairway to Heaven* by Led Zeppelin. I could not believe my eyes, or ears for that matter. My record player was playing *by itself*. Up until that point in my life, I thought that a stereo needed some human intervention to make it work—like someone turning it on and off.

It just played the last part of the song... *and she's buying a stairway to Heaven.*

*There is that Heaven theme again* I thought to myself. Someone was clearly trying to get my attention. I called Bryan immediately.

"Bryan, you're not going to believe what just happened..."

He believed it. He had been praying for me for eight months, and it was clear to him that God was at work.

"Hallelujah!" he said, "God is getting your attention." Indeed He was.

As an agnostic, I believed there might be a God, but my question was always, "Where is He?" Up until this time, it was very hard for me to believe that there was anything beyond humanity; if I could not see it, then it must not be real. But now

I understood that there was more to life than meets the *eye*—literally. Could there really be an unseen world all around me?

## DEAN BLACKSTONE

Two days later, one of my college friends, Dean Blackstone, gave me a ride to Richmond. In those days I had a *pharmaceutical* side business to supplement my meager income. I was going to buy some speed. In reality, they were just caffeine pills (Remember, I would take one before going to bag groceries at Safeway.) and perfectly legal but I would tell the unsuspecting yuppies at Louisburg that it was speed and sell the pills for a dollar apiece. They would feel like they'd just drunk five cups of coffee and everyone would be happy.

On the way back to Louisburg, Dean and I stopped at the Safeway grocery store where Jimmy worked. I wanted to say Hello to him before we went back. After seeing Jimmy, we got back into the car and I said to Dean, "That guy Jimmy is a born again Christian."

"I used to be one" Dean said.

*"WHAT?!"*

"I used to be a believer; I used to live that way."

"Dean, how do you *used to be* a believer???"

He explained to me that at one point in his life he was serving God. He used the words *used to* because although he still believed that Jesus was the Messiah and Son of God, he knew that truly believing meant letting God take control of your life and he was no longer willing to do that.

"Dean, what was your life like when you were a believer?" I asked. This was the one question I had to keep asking: Is serving Jesus boring? I needed to know.

Dean's face lit up with joy, just like Bryan's did only a few days earlier. He told me of the thrill of having a vibrant relationship with the Almighty. He was the second person to tell me that I could actually know God—in the span of five days, after going eighteen years without anyone telling me!

"What happened, Dean? Why would you give that up? Why have you turned your back on your faith?" I continued to probe. His expression went from fire to ice, as he told me how he had caved in to peer pressure and the desires of his friends.

We talked about God all the way back to school—for two solid hours. While we were talking, something strange happened; I began to feel good—*really good.* It was a feeling I had never felt before. For the first time in my life I was actually experiencing the presence of God. It is a feeling familiar to me now but at the time it was the most amazing peace I had ever known.

In addition to an incredible feeling of tranquility, something else happened. Suddenly, I could see myself as a believer. Before then, I could never see myself as *one of them.* I was Jewish—and believing in Jesus is not a Jewish thing to do—or so I thought. But now I knew what I wanted. I wanted God at any cost.

## E.T. AND MY EMOTIONS

Dean invited me—actually insisted—that I go with him to a movie on Thursday night in his hometown of Durham. He said it was about being a believer and I would find it interesting.

At the end of the movie I was crying. *You cry at movies all the time. This doesn't mean anything,* I told myself. (It was true. I did cry at movies all the time. My friends laughed at me when we saw *ET.* Tears streamed down my face as my heart ached for the Extra Terrestrial as he lay pale and gray, half-dead in the middle of a creek. You remember... his little flashlight heart thingy had stopped working.) I certainly wasn't going to make the most important decision of my life because a movie got to my emotions. I looked over and Dean was crying too.

## "AM I GOING TO DIE?"

After the movie Dean and I got into his car and started on our way home. I realized that my response to the movie might have been emotional, but it did get me thinking. I began to pray silently. I think this was the first time in my life that I honestly prayed to God.

*God, eight months ago I did not believe you were real. Now I do, but I need to know about Jesus. Is He the Messiah? I will serve you, whether it is through Jesus or Judaism. Just show me the truth!*

And suddenly, in the middle of my prayer—my first prayer—Dean lost control of the car. We began to swerve back and forth, side to side, and then the car started to spin around in circles. I remember thinking to myself, *Am I going to die?* In a split second, I realized how fragile my life was. One slip of the steering wheel and my life could be over. I could be facing God at any second and I still didn't know how to connect with Him. Our lives are delicate. At times we feel indestructible, but here I was, hanging in the balance between life and death—or so I thought. My only question was, *"Am I going to die?"*

And then a resounding "No!" reverberated on the inside of me. Something told me, "You will *not* die!" Then the car caught the ditch and flipped over one and a half times. The car was totaled, but miraculously neither Dean nor I had a scratch on us. Most people assume at this point that my near death experience caused me to become religious. Quite the contrary! My first thought, as we lay upside down in the car, was, *Jesus isn't real. If Jesus were real, this would not have happened!* Think about it. I am

80

praying, asking God to show me the truth and instead I almost die!

We got out of the car. I had to climb over the bottom of the car, which was now the top. Dean was pretty shaken up over totaling his car and almost getting us killed. As for me, finding out if Jesus was the Messiah was still my primary concern.

Fortunately there was a farmhouse within 100 yards from where we wrecked. We were on a narrow country road somewhere between Durham and Louisburg. We could easily have had to walk miles to the nearest house, yet here we were virtually right in front of one. We walked up and knocked on the door. A very friendly couple answered the door and invited us in.

I immediately noticed a Bible and some magazines that led me to think they might be believers. So, in my matter-of-fact style, I asked them and was really excited to find out that they were.

While the husband was helping Dean call the police and a tow-truck, the wife and I sat down.

"Listen," I said. "I am Jewish, and my best friend tells me I need to believe in Jesus, but if Jesus *was* the Son of God, why didn't He get off the cross and prove it?"

"He didn't come to *get off* the cross but to *die on* the cross," she replied.

This made no sense to me. "Why did He come to die?" I queried.

She went on to explain that Jesus, purposely, took on Himself the penalty of death, to pay the price for our sins. This further confused me, because I thought, *What's the big deal about sin? So I've stolen a few things, etc. Am I really such a bad guy?* I had already forgotten how bad I'd felt just a few months earlier when I realized that I had broken the seventh commandment.

My problem was that I was comparing myself to my friends, who were as bad, or worse than I was. As far as I was concerned, I was a good person. When I compared my life with God's standard, however, the Ten Commandments, I failed the test miserably and came up short.

# CHAPTER THIRTEEN

## GUILTY AS CHARGED

If you have read this far, please don't stop now. Before I finish the story I want to share a few thoughts along the lines of what this woman shared with me that night of the accident in North Carolina in 1983. These may be the most important few pages you will ever read.

Most people consider themselves basically good, with perhaps a few flaws. In fact, when I ask people the question, "Why would God let you into Heaven?" 95 percent give the same answer, *"Because I'm a good person."*

Ray Comfort, a Jewish believer in Jesus from New Zealand, told an interesting story. A girl once remarked how white her sheep looked against the green grass. (There are lots of sheep in New Zealand!) She went to sleep that night and it snowed. The next morning when she looked out the window, she thought how dirty the same sheep now looked against the white snow. The sheep hadn't changed; only the standard by which she judged its whiteness. If you compare yourself to *man's* standard of goodness, you will come up reasonably clean. If you measure yourself against your friends, you may appear really nice. When you compare yourself, however, to *God's* pure, snow-white standard of righteousness, your imperfections will be glaringly obvious.

After death, God will judge us. *"It is appointed for men to die once, and after this the judgment"* (Hebrews 9:27 NKJ). Our lives will be measured against the *Ten Commandments*. When I lined up my own life against these commandments, I realized it was an awful offense to God. I had made little to no effort to honor God's laws and without even knowing it, I had broken every one of His commandments. *What about you?* How do you measure up?

## 1.  YOU SHALL HAVE NO OTHER GODS BEFORE ME.

Do you love God with all your heart, soul, and strength? Is He the focal point of your affections? We are to love the Lord our God with all our heart, and with all our soul and with all our strength.

God is jealous for our love. In fact, He created you for the purpose of loving Him and receiving His love in return.

When I was in college, I once received a ride home from a girl in my class. The whole way back to Richmond, she kept talking about her dog, whom she had not seen in months. She adored her dog, and supposedly the dog adored her. When we arrived at her home, she hurried into the house to see her dog. To her surprise, the dog ran straight past her and began to jump up on me, as if I was its best friend. She was crushed.

Many of us are like that dog, not recognizing to whom we owe our affections. I was not the owner—I had not raised it from a pup—I never got up to let it outside at 5:00 a.m. and I didn't feed it every day—and yet the dog wrongly gave its affections to me. God is the one who created us and provides for us, yet we continue to put so many things before Him: sport, cars, career, ambitions, romantic interests, material possessions, our hobbies, etc, etc.

Personally, I had broken this commandment every day of my life. I didn't know Him, and worse—I didn't care.

## 2. YOU SHALL NOT MAKE FOR YOURSELF AN IDOL IN THE FORM OF ANYTHING...

While most of us don't literally bow down to idols as those involved in many pagan religions do, we can still be guilty of worshipping an idol. This commandment refers not only to idols made of wood or stone, but includes idols "in the form of anything," (Ex. 20:4) even idols which only exist *in our minds.*

Millions of people today create their own god according to their own conception of what God should be like.

Ray Comfort says:

> Many say, "*My* god is a god of love; He would never create Hell." The irony is, that they are right, their god would never create Hell, because he doesn't exist, he is a figment of their vain imagination, shaped to conform to their sins.[2]

In the Bible God says, "For my thoughts are not your thoughts, neither are your ways my ways" (Is. 58:8). We cannot simply decide *Who God is* and *what He should be like.* That is no different from creating an idol and worshiping it. The Bible alone reveals God to man, telling us exactly Who God is and what He is like.

When setting up new software on your computer, there is always a *preference menu* which Provides options for how you want the program to look and perform. Do you want spellcheck?

2    http://www.smithworks.org/evangelism/10_steps.html

What would you like your default font to be? God, however, does not come with a preferences menu. We are to conform to His preferences, not the other way around.

Simply because you say that you do or do not believe in something, does not make it real or not real. If you take a cyanide tablet believing it to be an aspirin, *you will still die!* You owe it to yourself to find out the truth.

## 3. YOU SHALL NOT MISUSE THE NAME OF THE LORD YOUR GOD, FOR THE LORD WILL NOT HOLD ANYONE GUILTLESS WHO MISUSES HIS NAME.

A young man is building a deck. He takes the hammer and although he is aiming for the nail, he hits his thumb. He is now going to express his pain and anger at himself for smashing his thumb with a hammer. The question is, *How will he do it?* He may reach way down for the most expressive, explicit, crude, four-letter word he can find.  Or He may take the most Holy Name there has ever been, the most precious Name there ever was, the Name that is above every name (Phil. 2:9)—the name of Jesus— and use it in place of a four-letter synonym for human excrement.

Not long ago my daughter and I were watching a movie. Suddenly one of the characters—in a moment when she should have been genuinely crying out to God, as she was caught cheating on her husband—looks at the man who is exposing her betrayal and yells at him: *Jesus Christ!*

I winced on the inside. Maybe for you, this is normal speech. I certainly hear it all the time. But just think about it. What if Jesus is the Messiah? What if He is the *Moshia*—Savior? How offensive to take the Name of Someone seeking to save you and turn it into a curse word! I mean, goodness, you don't hear people running around yelling *Mohamed* or *Buddha* when they are angry, but it is open season on the name of Jesus.

> Neither is there salvation in any other: for there is no other name under Heaven given among men, whereby we must be saved. (Acts 4:12)

I'm convinced Heaven shudders whenever anyone uses God's name in this derogatory way. I believe the angels tremble when they hear an ignorant earthling slander the Almighty in this crude manner. In fact, this is the only commandment that contains an addendum, a warning for the transgressor, that God *"will not hold anyone guiltless who misuses His name"* (Ex. 20:7).

There have been occasions when people have thoughtlessly used the Lord's name in vain in my presence. Then they say, "Oh, excuse me Ron, I didn't realize you were there," as if my presence mattered. I always reply, "You don't need to apologize to me, but there is One here Whom you don't see, and He is the one you have offended. You should apologize to Him."

## 4. REMEMBER THE SABBATH DAY BY KEEPING IT HOLY.

How many of us give one *hour* per week, much less one day per week to God? Under the Law of Moses a person was stoned to death for breaking the Sabbath.

God here is enjoining us to *remember* that our Creator rested from His labor on the seventh day and since we are made in His image, He is entitling us to the same right and privilege.

# 5. HONOR YOUR FATHER AND YOUR MOTHER, SO THAT IT MAY GO WELL WITH YOU AND YOU MAY LIVE LONG IN THE LAND THE LORD YOUR GOD IS GIVING YOU.

I still have painful memories of speaking terribly to my parents. I failed to recognize my indebtedness to them or their authority in my life. I didn't show them the respect and honor they deserved. All that mattered to me was that nothing and no one got in the way of my desire for fun.

I have spat out the words *I hate you* at them, all for the grand purpose of making them feel guilty for not allowing me to do something I wanted to do. I could go on and on giving examples of how badly I dishonored the two people who loved me the most as I was growing up.

This fourth commandment comes with a Promise—implying that those who *do not* honor their parents will not have a long life—*"so that you may live long."* One possible explanation for a shortened life could be that, like Sabbath breakers, rebellious children were stoned to death...

# 6. YOU SHALL NOT MURDER.

Many people's definition of *being good* is *not to have murdered someone*. You don't believe me? Then try asking someone if they think they are a good person. You will find they will invariably answer, "Yes, I am a good person—(adding the all-important caveat) *I've never killed anyone.*" Yet when we consider what Yeshua said about murder, we realize that we are all guilty of murder:

You have heard that it was said to those of old, "You
shall not murder," and whoever murders will be in
danger of the judgment. But I say to you that whoever
is angry with his brother without a cause shall be in
danger of the judgment. And whoever says to his
brother, "Raca!" shall be in danger of the council. But
whoever says, "You fool!" shall be in danger of Hell fire.
(Matthew 5:21-22 NKJ)

John, the disciple of Yeshua, adds, "Anyone who hates his
brother is a murderer, and you know that no murderer has eternal
life in him" (1 John 3:15).

You see, God looks not only at our actions, but also at our
thoughts. He equates hatred with murder. If you hate someone,
He says, you've murdered them in your heart. The next
commandment is the same.

That first passage comes from the most famous message
that Yeshua ever gave, *The Sermon on the Mount.* In it He takes the
commands of God and applies them to our heart. It is funny how
people will seek to portray the Old Covenant as harsh, and the
New Covenant as light. In this sermon Yeshua makes it clear that
all are guilty of breaking God's laws. Let's continue.

## 7. YOU SHALL NOT COMMIT ADULTERY.

Adultery is just like murder, in that if you think it, you've
as much as done it—and are GUILTY! Let's look at the words of
Yeshua.

You have heard that it was said, "Do not commit
adultery." But I tell you, that anyone who looks at a

woman lustfully has already committed adultery with
her in his heart. (Matthew 5:27-28)

In God's eyes if we lust after a woman, we've already
committed the sin in our heart. The book of Hebrews helps us
understand this:

For the word of God is living and active. Sharper than
any double-edged sword, it penetrates even to dividing
soul and spirit, joints and marrow; it judges the thoughts
and attitudes of the heart. Nothing in all creation is
hidden from God's sight. Everything is uncovered and
laid bare before the eyes of him to whom we must give
account. (Hebrews 4:12-13)

One day you and I will stand before a Holy God and all our
sinful thoughts will be exposed. The Torah, the Law of God, will
come to test us to see whether we are innocent or guilty—and
these Ten Commandments will be our jury.

You see, a natural sword can pierce your flesh, but the Word
of God is a sword that can cut right through to the soul, revealing
our deepest thoughts, motivations and intentions. This passage
indicates that we will stand before God naked—not physically, but
spiritually *"uncovered and laid bare before the eyes of him to whom we
must give account."*

Imagine yourself standing exposed before all creation. You
come before the Seat of Judgment with billions of people, and
all the angels of Heaven looking on. God comes and asks you to
give an account of your life. You claim that you are innocent, as
we all would—but the words are barely out of your mouth, when
a video of your life begins to play out on a super large screen
as the world looks on. You think to yourself, *Well at least I never
killed anyone.* And then in horror you realize that the video is not

portraying your actions in life but your thought-life!!! The lust, greed, jealousy, hatred, adultery, murder, idolatry, selfishness— it's all there. You beg God to turn it off, as you fall to your knees weeping in shame and guilt.

It is a horrible thought and will be an even more horrible reality.

# 8. YOU SHALL NOT STEAL.

From my early teens I developed a habit of taking things that did not belong to me. I was a thief. It is not a matter of how much I stole or what it was worth. Some items were so insignificant I cannot even remember them—but God does.

You see, most people think that we will be judged, not on whether or not we broke these laws, but on *the number of times that we broke them compared to others.* Imagine a thief standing before a judge. His defense is that he only stole $100, while other people he knows have stolen much more. Or he reasons with the judge that he only did it once and therefore is not *really* guilty.

Can you imagine a criminal using that defense? Imagine a murderer telling a judge, "My good deeds outweigh my bad deeds. Yes, I killed that person but there are nearly seven billion people on earth that I didn't kill." That murderer would go to jail, or worse, get the death penalty. So why do we expect God's justice to be less exacting than that of an upright earthly judge?

An episode of *Law and Order: Criminal Intent* highlights this point. Officer Eames captures her husband's killer. He has eluded the police for nearly a decade. He felt so badly about the death that he became an emergency room doctor, seeking to help people, trying to make amends.

When he realizes that they have DNA evidence against him he desperately pleads, "I save people; I've saved hundreds of lives!"

Eames rightly reproves him, "It doesn't make up for the one you took away."

No amount of good deeds and can erase a bad one. Furthermore, we wrongly assume that because God is silent, that our sins will not be held against us. We mistake God's patience for apathy. As Officer Eames said to the murderer: "What did you think—that this wouldn't catch up with you?"

Now how would you react if that judge felt sorry for the murderer of Officer Eames' husband? What if he just let him off? "I can see you have changed. You are now saving lives. You are free to go." There would be outrage at such injustice.

Imagine that the judge said, "You know, you have only killed one person and have helped so many more to live. You are really not a bad person. Your good deeds clearly outweigh your bad ones. The court finds you innocent."

I am quite sure that you, as well as the family of the murder victim and many others, would be outraged—and rightly so. Why then, do people imagine that God, the judge of all the earth, will likewise fail to administer justice to the guilty sinner?

## 9. YOU SHALL NOT GIVE FALSE TESTIMONY AGAINST (LIE ABOUT) YOUR NEIGHBOR.

Who among us has never lied or falsely accused someone? Again, compared to others, we may measure up relatively well; but compared to the Son of God, the Messiah, Who never once did any of these things, we all fall short. *'There is none who does good.'* (Ps. 14:1b)

# 10. YOU SHALL NOT COVET YOUR NEIGHBOR'S HOUSE. YOU SHALL NOT COVET YOUR NEIGHBOR'S WIFE, OR HIS MANSERVANT OR MAIDSERVANT, HIS OX OR DONKEY, OR ANYTHING THAT BELONGS TO YOUR NEIGHBOR.

Have you ever coveted something you could not afford? Have you ever wanted anything belonging to another; his talents, situation, job, car, his wife, or her husband? If so, you have broken the last and final commandment.

## GUILTY OR INNOCENT

Now let me ask you a simple question: If God were to judge you by this standard, on The Day of Judgment, would you be innocent or guilty?

The answer is obvious: Guilty! We would all be guilty. We have all broken every one of the Ten Commandments, if not in deed, then in thought. If an earthly judge would sentence a person for breaking a minor law, how much more will the "Judge of all the earth do right" (Genesis 18:25) and sentence you for breaking every one of His ten decrees?

Every one of us is a lawbreaker, even those who appear outwardly to be virtually faultless. For those who still cling to the idea that their good deeds can atone for their bad ones, James 2:10 pulls the rug out from under their feet:

> For whoever shall keep the whole Law and yet offend in
> one point, he is guilty of all. (James 2:10 KJV)

God's word is unequivocal; not one of us is innocent of wrongdoing as the rabbi shares, "*All have sinned* and fall short of the glory of God" (Romans 3:23)

And from the Hebrew Scriptures:

> Indeed, there is no one on earth who is righteous, no one who does what is right and never sins. (Eccl. 7:20)

> God looks down from Heaven on all mankind to see
> if there are any who understand, any who seek God.
> Everyone has turned away, all have become corrupt;
> there is no one who does good, not even one. (Ps. 53:2-3)

God is a God of justice. As a righteous Judge, He must administer justice to those who have broken His holy commandments. "The wages of sin is death" (Rom 6:23).

Fortunately for you, *and me,* the story doesn't end here. God is not only a God of *justice* but also a God of *mercy.* He has no pleasure in seeing people pass into Hell for all eternity.

> He is patient with you, not wanting anyone to perish,
> but everyone to come to repentance... (2 Peter 3:91)

He doesn't want any of us to be punished, though we all deserve it. God, in His great mercy has made a way of escape for us, from the penalty due our sins, in that He took the penalty of death that we deserved upon Himself.

Thus God has legally made a way for us all to escape His righteous judgment. Why? Because He loves us! It cost Him dearly to fix this problem, but the nature of His mercy demanded it. Let me explain...

# CHAPTER FOURTEEN

## GOD'S PLAN TO RESCUE YOU

If I had listened more during Hebrew School when I was a child, I may have had a better understanding of the concept of *blood sacrifice*. This concept is woven all throughout the Jewish Bible.

> For the life of a creature is in the blood, and I have given it to you to make atonement for yourselves on the altar; it is the blood that makes atonement for one's life. (Leviticus 17:11)

When Yeshua shed His blood and died on the cross, *He literally purchased us with His life.* The question is this: Why was He fit to pay for our sins, while we could not? If the emergency room doctor/murderer from the last chapter could not adequately make amends for his crime through good works, how can Yeshua atone for us? He was qualified to do so for two reasons:

## 1. HE WAS NOT BORN OF ADAM.

Jewish people wonder why Yeshua had to be born of a virgin. The reason is simple. Everyone born from Adam's seed has inherited a sinful nature. The Talmud refers to this as the *Evil Inclination*. The Jewish Bible teaches that the sin nature is transmitted genetically through the male line. God told Moses that the sins of the fathers are visited upon the children (See Ex. 34:7).

If Yeshua were born of man (i.e. had a human father) He would have had the same propensity to sin as we do. God, by His Spirit planted the seed in the virgin so Yeshua would be born without sin.

Being born with a sinful nature simply means that instead of having the nature of God, as Adam did when God created him, we are born with a natural bent or inclination toward sin. Anyone who has ever had children knows that without training, left to themselves, children consistently choose rebellion. Even before a baby can speak, it knows to disobey. In fact, the child has an innate tendency toward disobedience. Through discipline, a child learns how to behave. However, Yeshua was different—He was perfect.

This is why the angel told Joseph in a dream, "She [Miriam/ Mary[3]] will give birth to a son, and you are to give Him the name Yeshua (which means Salvation), *because He will save His people from their sins*" (Matthew 1:21). By the way, who were "His people" referred to here by the angel? I will give you a hint—it wasn't the Romans or the Egyptians. I told you this was a Jewish story.

## 2. HE NEVER SINNED.

Because He was not contaminated with the degenerate seed of Adam's fallen race, He had the ability to live a perfect life. The seed God planted in Miriam was pure and undefiled. You may be surprised to learn that Isaiah predicted that:

> The Lord himself shall give you a sign; Behold, *a virgin shall conceive*, and bear a son, and shall call his name Immanuel. (Isaiah 7:14 KJV)

---

3    Yeshua's mother's name was a Jewish one, Miriam, not Mary.

There are those in the rabbinic community who will tell you that the Hebrew word translated virgin here, *almah,* merely means *young woman.* However that can easily be refuted.

*Almah* is never used to describe a married woman, no matter how young she is. It is always used in reference to an *unmarried* woman. Unmarried women were virgins. If the woman had relations before marriage, it is hard to conceive that a promiscuous woman's pregnancy would be a miraculous sign from God, as the whole point of the passage is that, *"The Lord Himself will give you a sign."* Getting pregnant, whether married or not, would not be a significant sign.

In addition, Dr. Cyrus Gordon maintains that the Septuagint, the Greek Translation of the Hebrew Scriptures for Greek speaking Jews, translates this word as *virgin* long before Yeshua was born.[4]

Being born of God's seed and not Adam's enabled Yeshua to live a holy life; He never sinned. If Yeshua had ever sinned, He would have disqualified Himself as Messiah and Savior. In order to be *"the Lamb of God, who takes away the sin of the world"* (John 1:29), He would need to be perfect.

> When anyone brings from the herd or flock a fellowship offering to the LORD to fulfill a special vow or as a freewill offering, it must be *without defect or blemish to be acceptable.* (Lev. 22:21)

Yeshua never stole, never lusted, and never lied. He fulfilled the Torah, the Law of God, perfectly. Thus, when He went to the cross and laid down His life, He did so as a lamb *"without defect or blemish"* (Lev. 22:21).

Because He was perfect, He was qualified to die for our sins as our substitute. We see a picture of this in the Passover story. It

---

was the blood of an innocent lamb, spread upon the doorpost of each Israelite house that kept the Angel of Death away. *That blood* provided temporal protection. Yeshua's blood will protect us from eternal death and separation from God, and enable all who apply it to the doorposts of their heart to enter into God's Kingdom forever.

This is exactly what Isaiah, the Old Covenant prophet, told us Yeshua's sacrifice would accomplish:

> But He was *pierced* for our transgressions,
> He was crushed for our iniquities; the punishment that
> brought us peace was on Him, and by His wounds we
> are healed. (Isaiah 53:4)

Just before Yeshua died, He cried out, "'It is finished.' With that, he bowed his head and gave up his spirit" (John 19:30). When He said those words, *It is finished*, the Bible records, there was an earthquake.

> At that moment... the earth shook and the rocks split...
> When the centurion and those with him who were
> guarding Jesus saw the earthquake and all that had
> happened, they were terrified, and exclaimed, 'Surely he
> was the Son of God!' (Matthew 27:51,54)

Another very significant event happened at that moment. *"The curtain of the temple was torn in two from top to bottom"* (Mark 15:38). The curtain in the Temple separated an unholy people from a Holy God. If anyone went behind that curtain without permission from God, he would be struck down.

> Aaron's sons, Nadab and Abihu took their censers,
> put fire in them and added incense; and they offered
> unauthorized fire before the LORD, contrary to His

command. So fire came out from the presence of the
LORD and consumed them, and they died before the
LORD. (Leviticus 10:1-2)

The High Priest alone was ordained by God to enter into the
Holy of Holies, once a year, to offer the blood of atonement for the
sins of the nation.

The tearing of the curtain in the Temple from "top to bottom"
was a declaration from God that the barrier between God and
man had been removed—that Yeshua's blood was an acceptable
sacrifice for the sins of men.

> When the Messiah came as high priest... He did not
> enter by means of the blood of goats and calves; but he
> entered the Most Holy Place once, for all, by his own
> blood, having obtained eternal redemption (Hebrews
> 9:11a, 12)

No longer would there be a need for endless sacrifices for sin.
Yeshua had paid the price so that all men could be forgiven of their
sins and have free, unhindered access to God

> For we do not have a High Priest who cannot
> sympathize with our weaknesses, but was in all points
> tempted as we are, yet without sin. Let us *therefore come*
> *boldly to the throne of grace*, that we may obtain mercy and
> find grace to help in time of need. (Heb. 4:15-16 NKJ)

Notice how the curtain was torn, 'from top to bottom',
signifying that this was the work of God and not man. The Temple
curtain was reputedly four inches thick and twenty meters high,
making it an impossible feat for anyone other than God to rip
it. Yet it was ripped, signifying that Yeshua, the Messiah, had
paid the price for you to have eternal life and be forgiven and

cleansed from your sins. He had satisfied the demands of the Law: *"For without the shedding of blood there can be no forgiveness of sin"* (Hebrews 9:22b).

The Judge of all the earth had legally made a way for you to be forgiven, set free, and reconciled to Him.

------

Please take a moment and read the following prophecy of Isaiah, found in Chapter 53. More than any other Old Covenant passage, this prophecy, written over seven hundred years before Yeshua came, *describes Yeshua's mission in incredible detail.* In fact, a Jewish man who worked for me yelled at me when I read him this passage, saying, "Stop reading from the New Testament!" He was genuinely stunned to learn that this passage was, in fact, to be found in the Hebrew Scriptures.

## ISAIAH 53

¹ Who has believed our report?
And to whom has the arm of the LORD been revealed?
² For He shall grow up before Him as a tender plant,
And as a root out of dry ground.
He has no form or comeliness;
And when we see Him,
There is no beauty that we should desire Him.
³ He is despised and rejected by men,
A Man of sorrows and acquainted with grief.
And we hid, as it were, our faces from Him;
He was despised, and we did not esteem Him.

[4] Surely He has borne our griefs
   And carried our sorrows;
   Yet we esteemed Him stricken,
   Smitten by God, and afflicted.
[5] But He was wounded for our transgressions,
   He was bruised for our iniquities;
   The chastisement for our peace was upon Him,
   And by His stripes we are healed.
[6] All we like sheep have gone astray;
   We have turned, every one, to his own way;
   And the LORD has laid on Him the iniquity of us all.
[7] He was oppressed and He was afflicted,
   Yet He opened not His mouth;
   He was led as a lamb to the slaughter,
   And as a sheep before its shearers is silent,
   So He opened not His mouth.
[8] He was taken from prison and from judgment,
   And who will declare His generation?
   For He was cut off from the land of the living;
   For the transgressions of My people He was stricken.
[9] And they made His grave with the wicked—
   But with the rich at His death,
   Because He had done no violence,
   Nor was any deceit in His mouth.
[10] Yet it pleased the LORD to bruise Him;
   He has put Him to grief.
   When You make His soul an offering for sin,
   He shall see His seed, He shall prolong His days,
   And the pleasure of the LORD shall prosper in His hand.

[11] He shall see the labor of His soul, and be satisfied.
  By His knowledge My righteous Servant shall justify many,
  For He shall bear their iniquities.
[12] Therefore I will divide Him a portion with the great,
  And He shall divide the spoil with the strong,
  Because He poured out His soul unto death,
  And He was numbered with the transgressors,
  And He bore the sin of many,
  And made intercession for the transgressors.

# CHAPTER FIFTEEN

## NEW LIFE

Getting back to the story... Two things took place as I was listening to this woman share with me.

First, I recognized very clearly that I did not understand anything she was talking about. *Blood... Sacrifice... death... sin?*

And second, despite my lack of understanding, I was experiencing the most powerful force I ever felt—and it was all over me. I tried to resist this power, wondering what it was, realizing that it was far stronger than mere emotion; but the more I resisted, the deeper it became. This lasted for quite some time.

Believe me, please, *I am not making this up*—I was experiencing the power of God. It was awesome! This force was more powerful than any drug I ever took. It was pure and wonderful. (I have been a believer for nearly thirty years now and I regularly experience that same feeling, although not to the same intensity. It *is* the presence of God.) To this day, I have not found words that are adequate to describe this experience. At the time I remember thinking there was a force field of electricity or energy coming off of my body about 18 inches in every direction.

It was at that moment, in the midst of feeling the very presence of God, that I realized that this was REAL! That *He* was REAL!!!

God had convinced me: *the movie, the car wreck—right in front of the home of these people who were believers—and now this awesome power.* I surrendered. God had won.  How could I say "no" when He had answered my simple, but sincere prayer—*Show me the truth*—so radically!

Once I acknowledged that I was a sinner and I needed Yeshua, I was changed immediately. I was new on the inside. I had never felt this way before. It was wonderful, and at the same time strangely unfamiliar. It was all totally new to me.

According to the Scriptures I had been *born again.* When I was born naturally I had taken my first breath of air. But this birth was *spiritual.* The life of God was breathed into my spirit. The forgiveness I had searched for on Yom Kippur just one month earlier was now mine… and it came as a gift from the Jewish man, Yeshua.

That same evening the husband drove us back to Louisburg. I don't remember much of our conversation. When we got back to school (which was well after midnight) and told everyone what had happened, some of them wanted to see the car. So Bernie, Philip, Dean, and I drove out to the pound where they'd taken the car. It was smashed! The car was totaled, but we were not.  The whole way back to school I shared non-stop with these guys about my new-found faith. It was all I cared about.

## A NEW DAY, A NEW LIFE

The next day was thrilling. It was the beginning of a brand new life. Old habits just disappeared. No one told me to stop cussing; I simply could not speak those words anymore. Before I was a believer, I had a mouth like a sailor. Curse words were a part of my normal vocabulary—and now I couldn't even hear them without cringing. When someone is *born again*, they receive a new nature and power over sin. Old habits are conquered by the power of Yeshua's Spirit. Yeshua does not save you from your sins and then leave you in them; He sets you free and gives you power to overcome destructive behavior. When you make Yeshua the Lord of your life, you are transformed from the inside by the awesome power of God.

> Therefore, if anyone is in Messiah, he is a new creation; the old has gone, the new has come! (2 Corinthians 5:17)

The Jewish prophet Ezekiel spoke of this change of heart hundreds of years before Yeshua came. In fact, he prophesied that this will happen en masse to the Jewish people after we have returned to the Land of Israel (the Jewish homeland which declared statehood in 1948).

> For I will take you out of the nations; I will gather you from all the countries and bring you back into your own land. I will sprinkle clean water on you, and you will be clean; I will cleanse you from all your impurities and from all your idols. I will give you a new heart and put a new spirit in you; I will remove from you your heart of stone and give you a heart of flesh. And I will put my Spirit in you and move you to follow my decrees and be careful to keep my laws. (Ezekiel 36:26-27)

I called Bryan on the phone. He was overjoyed. He told me he would drive down to Louisburg that night and take me back to Richmond for the weekend. I knew he wouldn't arrive until late, so I went out to a bar with my friends.

Grace was a young lady who had become a close friend of mine. She had been trying for some time to introduce me to her girlfriend from Wilmington, but it had never worked out. Of all times, this was the night that her friend was there. We were introduced and I didn't think twice about it. I was devoid of any desire to pursue the relationship. It wasn't that she was unattractive, but that I was serving a different master now.

"Ron, what's the matter? Don't you like her? She likes you," Grace queried, a bit of concern in her voice. I thought to myself, *She 'likes' me. She doesn't even know me! I could be an ax-murdering rapist—and she says she likes me! How ridiculous!*

"Grace, come outside with me for a moment." When we got outside the bar, I explained to her what had happened to me from beginning to end. When I finished she had tears in her eyes. She then confessed to me that she had accepted Jesus when she was younger, but like Dean, had chosen her friends and her current lifestyle over God. I have no doubt that God was offering *the grace to change,* to Grace at that moment. Sadly she rejected it and she entered into a promiscuous lifestyle, which was far worse than her previous lifestyle.

Bryan finally showed up, and I was thrilled to see that my old friend, Chris Miller, was with him. Of course Chris was not a believer and was accompanied by a six-pack of Budweiser. I talked them both into going to a party not far away before we went home. I was offered a beer when I walked in and I declined. *When has anybody ever offered me a free beer?* I thought to myself.

This was my first night as a new creation in Messiah and already I was being offered girls and booze! This did not happen before I was a believer. But it didn't matter—I wasn't interested. I had found something better—something far more satisfying.

*(Don't get me wrong, I'm not saying that drinking a beer is wrong. You have to understand that besides being underage, I looked upon alcohol solely as a means of getting drunk—that was it. Plus, I was drinking nearly every day. So for me, at that time, alcohol was a problem and it was time to quit. Now, that I'm living in Israel where a glass of wine is often served at meals, it is a very different culture from that of my*

*teenage years. I never knew then that people could actually have a glass of wine without needing to finish the bottle!)*

It didn't take me long to realize that this party and these people had nothing to offer me. I grabbed Bryan and Chris and we left abruptly.

As we drove back to Richmond, Bryan began to pray. "In the name of Jesus!" he said fervently. Immediately in the back seat Chris said, "What was that? Did you feel that?" We pulled over and he dumped out all his beer. I don't know what he felt, but it was powerful enough to make him relinquish his six-pack— something we didn't do lightly in those days. (Remember earlier, John Harrington unwilling to get rid of our beer—even with the police on the way!)

The next week at school was exciting… and difficult. I told everyone about Jesus. I wanted everyone to know the truth. It was like, as Yeshua said, *being born again.* Everything felt new. It was as if I had been asleep, and something or someone finally woke me up.

I still had the bottle of caffeine pills that I had bought in Richmond. I asked some guys if they wanted to buy them from me, and they declined. Then I realized that it wouldn't be right to sell the pills, so I flushed them down the toilet. That night at dinner, Clay came over to me to inquire about the pills. Clay was over six feet tall, strong, and a total jerk. He was very intimidating as well. When I told him that I'd flushed the pills, he said, "You did what?" He continued to berate me until I took my tray and left. *Jesus, I am going to need your help if I am going to make it,* I prayed.

# CHAPTER SIXTEEN

## NO ONE TOLD ME THE NEW COVENANT WAS JEWISH!

As a new believer in Yeshua I began to read the Bible, starting in the New Covenant with the book of John. The more I read the New Covenant, the more surprised I became at how Jewish it was. This story didn't take place in Rome, there is no mention of the Vatican or the Pope and the word *Christian* only appears twice in the entire book! These people weren't starting a new religion—they were observant Jews who believed they had found their Messiah and had entered into the promised 'New Covenant' with the House of Israel. I was stunned to see that Jeremiah the Jewish prophet spoke of the New Covenant hundreds of years before Yeshua.

> "The time is coming," declares the Lord, "when I will make *a new covenant with the house of Israel and the house of Judah*." (Jer. 31:31)

In fact, it came as a total shock to me to discover that Gentiles didn't even begin to believe in Yeshua until a number of years after Yeshua rose from the dead. *Did you know that?* The entire following of Yeshua for roughly the first ten years after His resurrection was Jewish! It didn't even cross their minds to relate to, let alone reach out to, non-Jews. This was, after all, the fulfillment of *Jewish* prophecy. So, they naturally assumed that only Jews could believe in the Jewish Messiah.

Here are a few other facts I found out about the New Covenant that I think may surprise you.

1. Jesus' actual name is Yeshua. Yeshua comes from the Hebrew noun Yeshu-á, which means *salvation*. When the angel visited Joseph, he was told that he must give the child the name Yeshua, because He would bring salvation—*Yeshu-á*—to His people. He would "save" them "from their sins!" (Matt. 1:21) You miss this powerful prophetic wordplay in the Greek and English.

2. His mother's name was not Mary or even Maria. She was not Catholic! Her name was Miriam, and it is a Jewish name; the same name as the sister of Moses.

3. John (Yochanan) was not a Baptist. No disrespect to my Baptist friends, but John was the last and greatest of the Hebrew prophets in company with Jeremiah, Isaiah and Ezekiel. His was the prophesied "voice in the wilderness" (Is. 40:3) preparing his people for the coming of their Jewish Messiah, the Lamb of God.

4. Baptism is not unique to the New Testament. It holds an integral place in Judaism. Jews, practiced water immersion centuries before John began to baptize his Jewish followers. One of the reasons they responded so readily was because it was a familiar part of their culture. Archaeologists have discovered nearly 50 immersion tanks (mikvot), which were used for ritual cleansing before sacrifices were offered at the Temple. With the destruction

of the Temple, immersion was not emphasized as much, and with the horrific forced baptisms of Jews, by ill-informed so-called Christians, Jews have been left with a bad taste in their mouths regarding baptism. But make no mistake... it started with the Jewish people.

5.  Peter was NOT the first Pope! Peter (Kefa) was a Jew, and initially the leader of the first Jewish believers. He turned over the reins to Jacob, the brother of Yeshua in order to take the message of *salvation through Yeshua* to the Jews scattered abroad. There is zero evidence that Peter was ever the Bishop of Rome (title of Pope) or that he passed such a mantle to anyone else. Catholicism did not even step onto the stage of history until several centuries later.

6.  James is not the name of the fellow who wrote the Book of James and led the first Jewish believers in Acts 15. James might be a wonderful English name for a butler, a chauffeur or even a king... but NOT for a Jew in the first century. His name was actually Jacob (Ya'akov)!

7.  Another common misunderstanding is that Saul, on becoming a believer changed his Jewish name, Shaul to Paul, but this too is not so. The Bible merely mentions the fact that Saul was *also* called Paul (Acts 13:9) Like many Jews, he had a name common to the people amongst whom he lived as well as his Hebrew name. The idea that he ever traded his Jewish name for a gentile one is unbiblical and quite frankly, insulting. I too was given an English name, Ron, and a Hebrew one, Chaim, when I was born.

8. The entire New Testament was written by Jews! There is some debate on as to whether or not Luke was Jewish, but we know for a fact twenty out of the twenty-two books of the New Testament were penned by Jews—and possibly all twenty-two!

9. Communion was instituted at a Passover Seder. Yeshua picked up the Afikomen, the middle piece of matzah (unleavened bread) used during the Passover Seder and broke it, saying, "This is my body broken for you". Similarly, He lifted the third cup of four that are blessed during the Passover meal, the Cup of Redemption, and declared, "This is my blood of the covenant, which is poured out for many for forgiveness of sins" (Matt. 26:28). Everyone at that table was Jewish.

10. All of the original followers of Yeshua were Jewish. And when Gentiles began to believe in the *Jewish Messiah,* there were many Jews who felt these non-Jews needed to convert to Judaism first. A council was eventually convened to settle the issue (Acts 15) and it was decided that Gentiles didn't need to convert. But never did it enter the minds of the Jewish followers of Yeshua that they were no longer Jewish!

## PASSOVER, FIRST FRUITS AND SHAVUOT

It is also important to note that Yeshua rose from the dead NOT at Easter but on the Feast of Firstfruits. In fact, the three most significant events in the New Covenant all took place on Jewish Holy Days.

1.  **Yeshua died on Passover.** The last supper was actually the *last Seder.* (A Seder is the meal on the first night of Passover.) Yeshua celebrated Passover with His disciples, and the next morning He was killed.

2.  **Yeshua rose from the dead on *Bikurim*, Firstfruits.** The Bible teaches that the first Sunday after the first Shabbat of Passover marks the Feast of Firstfruits, a time of thanksgiving to God for the firstfruits of the harvest. This is why Paul (Saul) referred to Yeshua as "Messiah, the first fruits" (1 Cor. 15:23a) the "first born from among the dead" (Col. 1:18). How fitting that God should choose this day of all days to bring forth the Messiah from the grave.

3.  **The outpouring of the Holy Spirit on the first Jewish believers happened on Shavuot** or 'the day of Pentecost' as it is more commonly called in some quarters. Pentecost is a Greek word meaning *fifty.* Jews would count the days from Firstfruits to Shavuot. Shavuot means *weeks,* as in seven weeks or forty-nine days. Most Christians, when they read their Bibles, have no idea that this is a much-celebrated Jewish feast day commemorating the giving of the law to Moses.

How amazing that these three momentous events: the sacrificial death of God's Son, His resurrection, and the outpouring of the Holy Spirit (birthing the first assembly of Jewish believers -Acts 2), should all take place on these three auspicious Jewish Feasts. What are the chances of this happening? Want to the see the odds? This link will take you to an article I wrote on the topic: http://roncan.net/POeCvs

One seldom hears mention of it but there was a great spiritual revival in Jerusalem in the first century. It began during Yeshua's three years of teaching and doing miracles, which touched every nook and cranny of Judea and the Galilee. Many Jewish leaders embraced the message of Yeshua.

> So the word of God spread. The number of disciples in Jerusalem increased rapidly, and a *large number of priests* (*Kohanim*) and Jewish religious leaders became obedient to the faith. (Acts 6:7)

When Paul came to meet Jacob (James) and the other leaders in Jerusalem, the Bible says:

> On hearing it, they praised God; but they also said to him, "You see, brother, *how many tens of thousands of believers there are among the Jews*, and they are all zealots for the Torah." (Acts 20:21)

# CHAPTER SEVENTEEN

## IS JESUS ONLY FOR THE JEWS?

As I explained earlier, I assumed when I became a believer in Yeshua that I was no longer Jewish. I had been led to believe that following Yeshua meant that I had to turn my back on my family, my religion, my heritage and community. No one had ever actually said as much to me, but that is what I believed based on all I'd learned of Christianity and Judaism during my first eighteen years on the planet.

This was very a troubling issue for me because the last thing I wanted to do was hurt those close to me. And the truth is, I loved being Jewish; not from a religious point of view, but because I loved my culture and was proud of being Jewish, despite the fact that the whole world seems to be against us.

So I was surprised *and* relieved to read in the fifteenth chapter of the book of Acts that the first Jewish believers in Yeshua recognized Him as their Jewish Messiah—the One Isaiah had prophesied would be rejected, killed and raised to life again (Isaiah 53). There was no conflict of faith in their minds.

If you had told any of the leaders of this new Messianic Jewish experience that they had abandoned Judaism for a new religion, they would have thought you were crazy. The New Covenant doesn't even hint at such a notion.

*We are following Israel's long promised Messiah—what could be more Jewish than that?*

If you had asked them about Christianity, they would have asked, "What is Christianity?" Everything they believed was sourced in the Torah, the Prophets and the Psalms—the Hebrew Scriptures, which were the only Scriptures they had at that point in time.

> However, I admit that I worship the God of our fathers as a follower of the Way, which they call a sect. I believe everything that agrees with the Law and that is written in the Prophets, and I have the same hope in God as these men, that there will be a resurrection of both the righteous and the wicked. So I strive always to keep my conscience clear before God and man. (Acts 24:14-16)

> Then Paul made his defense: "I have done nothing wrong against the Jewish law or against the temple or against Caesar." (Acts 25:8)

All the first believers in Yeshua were Jewish, and their Jewishness was *never* in question.

## CAN A GENTILE BELIEVE IN JESUS WITHOUT BECOMING JEWISH?

You may think this is a bizarre question, and today it is. But that was precisely the subject of the first theological controversy among the early Jewish believers. Now, while I said that the Jewish believers' faith was never in question, there was quite a bit of confusion when the Gentiles *wanted in* on the Jewish Messiah. For the first several years, the Jerusalem congregation only shared the message of Yeshua with Jewish people. It never entered their minds to go to the Gentiles.

It wasn't until approximately ten years after the original Jerusalem revival at Shavuot around 30 CE that Gentiles began to receive salvation. And when Gentiles eventually did receive Yeshua, some were told they must also embrace Judaism.

This began with Simon Peter. The Lord instructed him to go to the home of a Roman named Cornelius. Cornelius himself had been visited by an angel and was told to send men for Peter. Peter was reluctant to go with them because he had never been in the home of a non-Jew. However, he was quite sure the Spirit of God was leading him.

Peter begins to speak:

> I now realize how true it is that God does not show favoritism but accepts from every nation the one who fears him and does what is right. You know the message God sent to the people of Israel, announcing the good news of peace through Yeshua the Messiah, who is Lord of all. (Acts 10:34-36)

This is the first time in nearly ten years of full time preaching that Peter is preaching to non-Jews. This is an eye-opener to him—that God wants to reach non-Jews! Notice two things he says here:

1. God does not show favoritism. He accepts men from every nation.
2. The message of salvation through Yeshua was sent to the people of Israel.[5]

How strange this all sounds to those of us who have been taught you can't be Jewish and believe in Jesus. Here is an Israelite making it clear that this whole thing started with

5 Jeremiah 31:31; Matt 15:24; John 4:22b

Israel and *that he himself is dumbfounded* that God should now be extending this salvation to the gentiles!

This next part is even more amazing:

> While Peter was still speaking these words, the
> Holy Spirit came on all who heard the message. The
> circumcised (Jewish) believers who had come with Peter
> were astonished that the gift of the Holy Spirit had been
> poured out even on Gentiles... Then Peter said, "Surely
> no one can stand in the way of their being immersed
> in water. They have received the Holy Spirit just as we
> have." So he ordered that they be immersed in the name
> of Yeshua the Messiah. (Acts 10:44-48)

Why do I find this so amazing? Well, Jewish people are particularly sensitive to the act of baptism or immersion and with good reason. During the Dark Ages, Jews were often forced by the Church to be baptized or face expulsion from their countries and in some cases Jews who refused baptism were even killed.

In 1189, when discussing whether or not Jewish converts to Christianity should be allowed to return to Judaism, the Archbishop of Canterbury declared, "If he (the Jew) desired to return to worship the devil he should be given free choice."[6]

The Church often referred to Judaism as demonic and compared it to witchcraft. Jews who accepted baptism during the Inquisitions had to read a public confession denouncing Judaism. If one of these *converts* was caught doing anything Jewish— lighting Shabbat candles or refusing to eat pork—he or she could be arrested by the Church and burned at the stake. Thousands of Jews died in this way.

---

6      http://www.jewishvirtuallibrary.org/jsource/judaica/ ejud_0002_0003_0_01984.html

Centuries of forced baptism of Jews by Gentiles certainly show how far the Church had diverged from its original calling to reflect the light of God to the world.

Here we see Peter after (1) a vision, (2) instruction from the Holy Spirit, (3) a visitation by angels to Cornelius and (4) the power of God falling on the crowd while he spoke, come to the conclusion that Gentiles could be baptized and become members of the body of believers—*without converting to Judaism.* Whereas one day earlier he would not have even considered setting foot in Cornelius's house, he is now joyfully immersing the whole household in water, as brothers and sisters in the Messiah.

Contrast his feelings as a Jewish believer in the Messiah to what I went through as a new believer. I wasn't struggling with the question of whether or not Gentiles could embrace the *Jewish* Messiah, but rather, whether I, as one born Jewish, could believe in Jesus and still be Jewish. How things have changed! (By the way, this conflict led to the writing of Identity Theft, my novel to be released in April 2013 by Destiny Image. For more information, please go to www.IDTheftBook.com.)

Getting back to the first century.... As other Messianic Jews began to share the Messiah with Gentiles there arose the belief that they must first be circumcised and convert to Judaism. Isn't that amazing!? I bet you never knew that. Jewish believers in Jesus told Gentiles, "You must first convert to Judaism if you want *in* on our Messiah!"

> Certain people came down from Judea to Antioch
> and were teaching the believers: "Unless you are
> circumcised, according to the custom taught by Moses,
> you cannot be saved." (Acts 15:1)

To make a long story short, a meeting was finally called in Jerusalem to settle the matter once and for all. The Messianic Jewish leaders met together and prayed. They asked God, and I paraphrase, "What do we do with all these Gentiles? What are the conditions of their admittance into the faith?"

It was finally decided that they should "not make it difficult for the Gentiles who are turning to God" (Acts 15:19). The Gentiles could believe in Yeshua without embracing the liturgy of the Torah.

Faith in Yeshua was so inarguably and incontrovertibly Jewish, that it was the prospect of Gentile membership, which posed a problem for the leadership.

# CHAPTER EIGHTEEN

## YOU'RE SUCH A NICE JEWISH BOY, HOW COULD YOU DO THIS TO YOUR PARENTS?

As a Jewish believer, the two questions I am asked over and over again are: "What is a nice Jewish boy like you doing believing in Jesus?" and secondly, "What did your parents think?"

I've spent the better part of this book answering the first question. Let me now answer the second one.

Halfway through the first week, I found out that John Harrington had called my parents. He'd told them he was worried about me because I had quit drinking and believed in Jesus. I was furious! I couldn't believe he'd done this.

As upset as I was, this actually turned out to be a blessing in disguise. I knew I needed to tell my parents, but I had no idea how I was going to do it. I knew it would break their hearts; that they wouldn't understand. Who knows how long it would have taken me to work up the courage? Like ripping off a Band-Aid, it was done.

## A VISIT FROM MOM AND DAD

They came down to Louisburg that weekend for Parents' Day. We sat down in my room, and I broke the ice by telling them I knew that John had called them. We had a good, if tense, talk. I told them what I believed and why. I showed them several passages in the Bible that had helped me make my decision.

They assumed it was a phase I was going through and that I would soon come to my senses. And why shouldn't they have thought this? *I had quit everything else I had ever started.* Why would this be any different?

## SHORT-LIVED FAITH?

For a while it looked like they might be right. Within a week or so I was drinking and doing drugs again. Although I knew what had happened to me was real, it was very difficult living it out *by myself.* I did not have any friends at college who were believers. There were temptations all around me... and eventually I gave in. This is why Yeshua sent out his disciples *two by two* and why it was written of Adam, that "It is not good for the man to be alone" (Gen. 2:18). I didn't need a wife, but a good friend would have helped.

The early Jewish believers met together regularly for mutual encouragement and worship. I had nobody. Like Dean, I still believed in Jesus, but I was not letting Him have full control of my life. My biggest problem was that news about my newfound relationship with Jesus had spread like wildfire. All of my friends in Richmond knew.

When the semester ended and I went home to Richmond, I spent a lot of my time saying, "Yes, I believe in Jesus, but I am still the same guy." I wanted everyone to know that I was still the *fun guy* they used to know. Of course, when someone has met Yeshua, they should not be telling everyone they are still the same; they should be telling everyone, "I WILL *NEVER* BE THE SAME AGAIN!"

For the next couple of months I drank, did drugs, and partied just like I used to. I ended up dropping out of Louisburg because my parents would not buy me a car. I told them I was not going back to school without a car. I didn't really mean it at first, but when they called my bluff, I dug in my heels and impulsively dropped out of Louisburg.

That turned out to be one impulsive decision that really worked out. The chances of my following God while at Louisburg were slim. I was constantly surrounded by drugs and alcohol and was not strong enough on my own to resist. And to be clear, it wasn't just the availability of drugs and alcohol that tripped me up. It was the lack of friendship with other committed believers. In Richmond, I had constant contact with other believers.

## A SECOND CHANCE

In February of 1984, Bryan asked me to go to a concert. At the end of the concert, Leon Patillo, a well-known gospel singer formerly of the rock band *Santana*, asked if there was anyone there who wanted to *re*dedicate his or her life to the Lord. Bryan asked me if I wanted to stand, and I did. I wanted Yeshua, but I was still not willing to give Him everything. "God, I am going to serve You," I said—*"half way.* I will start attending a congregation, but I am still going to drink and go to parties"

I actually said that! *Halfway!* Nobody told me God doesn't make halfway deals. The deal of all deals was made when His Son gave His *whole* life for me. How could I give him only *half* of mine in return?

The next night I found myself with Mike White, snorting cocaine. We split a gram and went out to a bar. For some reason the drug did not affect me. Cocaine is very expensive and I knew this was good stuff because Mike was enjoying it. *I could not feel anything*, so I continued to get drunk. Finally, realizing that it had been a miserable evening, I went out to my car to go home. I was driving down Patterson Avenue thinking what a lousy evening it had been when suddenly I heard a voice. "Ron, if you had had a good time tonight, you never would have come back to Me."

I don't know what happened at that moment, but something exploded on the inside of me. I screamed out, "I surrender, I surrender! You have my life, my whole life. I will serve You the rest of my days..." It was as if I had been arrested. I was instantly filled with the presence of the Lord. I knew this was different. In the split second that God spoke to me, I was set free.

There is an old Don Francisco song about a man in Matthew, chapter nine, whose daughter is raised the dead by Yeshua. It 's called, *I Gotta Tell Somebody*. That is how I felt. I had to tell somebody! I drove to a friend's apartment to see if any of my buddies was there so I could talk to them about Yeshua. Miles Jones, whom we affectionately called *Barney Rubble*, was sitting on the front porch by himself. He looked extremely depressed and I ended up sharing with him for almost an hour about what God had done in my life. Many years later he recognized me in front of a grocery store and I was able to give him a copy of this book! (The first edition.)

Then I drove to Jimmy's house, but he wasn't at home. *Maybe Bryan is home,* I thought. So I went to his house, but he was also out. I finally just went home, but I couldn't sleep so I called Jimmy at 2 a.m. and we talked for an hour. Then I called Bryan at 3 a.m.

The next night I went with both of them to Grace Street in downtown Richmond, where I used to hang out. When I was partying there, I wouldn't even walk on the side of the street where the biker bar stood. Now here I was standing nonchalantly in front of *Hababa's*! In fact, we talked to the bikers about Jesus.

A supernatural boldness came over me that was unreal. I wasn't afraid of anything. Before I was a believer, I was so fearful.

You'll recall how I had chickened out of a fight in high school. And here I was confidently getting in the face of guys with tattoos (Back then, if you had a tattoo you were most likely pretty tough—now housewives have them!) and Harley-Davidsons (I guess the same could be said about Harleys. Now every rich guy has his Harley, but in 1983 it was different).

Instead of being ashamed of my faith, I wanted everyone to know about it. I figured if I was loud and crazy before, why should I be anything less for Yeshua? If as an unbeliever I was willing to look foolish, why shouldn't I be as willing to be bold for my faith? I had the Son of God backing me up now; before I was alone. People paint their bodies and take off their shirts in zero-degree weather to cheer for their favorite football team, and we think nothing of it—*They're just having fun expressing themselves.* Yet, we think it strange when a believer expresses even half that amount of passion about his relationship with God. Honestly, shouldn't we get more excited about the Creator of the heavens and the earth, Who wants to have relationship with us, than we do about the Cowboys or the Yankees—most of whom care very little about their fans?

I began to tell all my old friends about Jesus. If I had a free night, I might go to a bar where the kids I went to high school with were hanging out. I would go from table to table, telling them what had happened to me.

During that first week I'd wondered if I had the strength to leave my old life for good. Drugs, alcohol and my old friends were so much a part of my life that I knew it was just a matter of time before I returned. But one week quickly turned into two, and two into three, then a month had gone by, two months, and so it went on. With each passing day I grew stronger and stronger in my love for God and my abhorrence of my old life.

Having friends like Bryan and Jimmy helped a lot. Without their encouragement and friendship, I do not think I would have made it. We did everything together.

I made some new friends as well, James Brewer, Scott Brindley, Steve Raymond, Mike Reynolds and Gary Stergar. Gary was a defensive lineman for the University of Richmond. Steve played safety. Gary was a gentle giant, a humble man totally dedicated to his faith.

Then there was Bob Smith. Bob was the youth pastor at River of Life Church in Richmond. To tell the truth, Bob was more like a *drill sergeant* than a youth pastor. (He would approve of that description of his character.) There was no fluff with Bob. He was forty, graying and tough as nails—clearly old school. He had just what this Jewish boy needed.

I was used to calling all my parents' friends by their first names. However, Bob was *Mr. Smith!* He taught me how to respect authority—and a few hundred other things as well…

He taught us the Bible into the wee hours of the night. We went over to his house several nights a week just to hang out with his family. Vickie, his wife, often kicked us out around one o'clock in the morning—sometimes later.

Bob was a great example to us. He always shared his faith and had personally led many of the people in our congregation to Yeshua. His license plate read "JOHN 33." People would say, "I thought your name was Bob, not John." Without missing a beat, Bob would reply, "You must be born again." (John 3:3 is a passage in the New Covenant where Yeshua says that you must be born again.) Bob not only taught us the faith, he lived it out in front of us.

## SUMMER AND THE BEACH

As summer approached, I decided to go to the beach with Eddie and Page for our annual beach week. This year would be different. Instead of getting wasted for a week, strung out on LSD, I was now on a mission: To tell all my old friends from high school what Jesus had done in my life. The drive down to Virginia Beach felt strange. It was weird not being accompanied by a six-pack of Budweiser. I stayed down there for a few days, sleeping on floors and in the back seats of cars. I shared the Gospel with everyone I knew. I wish more of them had been open to the Lord. I still pray for all my classmates in Mils E. Godwin's class of '83... for Eddie, John, Mike, Chris, and Jackie and the list goes on. Thanks to Facebook, I have reconnected with many of them and it's been so great to discover some of my classmates have come to faith!

Bryan, Jimmy, James, Gary, and I began going to the toughest parts of Richmond to talk to people about eternity. I remember one time the five of us went into a White Tower restaurant. If you don't know what White Tower is, you may have White Castle— the lowest form of fast-food ever created. It makes McDonald's look like Ruth's Chris Steak House. It was filled with prostitutes and homeless people.

"I'd like to share a story with you. It's about how I came to know Jesus. I..." No one blinked an eye. No one told me to shut up either; they simply ignored me. I determined that their rejection wasn't going to deter me. "I think we will talk to each of you individually," I said. Jimmy sat next to a prostitute and began to talk to *her*. As the prostitute turned to address Jimmy, *a man's voice came out*. It didn't take Jimmy more than a second to realize that *she* was a *he*!

# CHAPTER NINETEEN

## BRINGING IN THE BIG GUNS—"THE BUTCHER" AND RABBI FINE

In the first year after I embraced Yeshua. I had two intense encounters with Orthodox rabbis. Rabbi Immanuel Schochet was a Lubavitcher, a sect of Orthodox Judaism based in Brooklyn (widely known for proclaiming their leader in the nineties, Menachem Mendel Schneerson, to be the Messiah— even after his death) trained specifically to *deprogram* people like me while Yehuda Fine, from Brooklyn, was an Orthodox Jewish family therapist who spent a good deal of his time working with Messianic Jews. Rabbi Immanuel Schochet's style was completely the opposite of Yehuda's, but their goal was the same: destroy my faith. Schochet relied on intimidation, while Yehuda relied on manipulation. In Yehuda's defense, I don't think he would call it manipulation, but seeking to relate to me, as the rabbi refers to himself on his website as "America's most *streetwise* family and teen expert." More on that in minute—let's start with *The Butcher*.

Rabbi Schochet came to town from Canada. He visited Jewish communities all over the United States and Canada warning Jews to stay away from believers. Rabbi Schochet is like a modern-day Saul of Tarsus—prior to Saul's acceptance of Yeshua. His life's mission was to keep Jewish people from believing in Yeshua. That may sound noble to some Jewish people. However, his methods were anything but noble.

Years after my meeting with Schochet, I met a young Lubavitch Jew named Ya'akov who had come to believe in Yeshua. Ya'akov told me how he'd been kidnapped and taken to Canada, where he met with these deprogrammers. Schochet was one of the leaders of the program. For nine days they gave him only bread and juice. He finally told them that he didn't believe in Yeshua anymore, just so they would release him. A few days after I met and spoke with Ya'akov, he was out taking a walk when a car pulled up beside him. Several orthodox Jewish men jumped out and grabbed him. They kidnapped him again, but this time, using false passports, they took him to Israel. Once there, with the help of a willing doctor, they kept him drugged. For how long, I am not sure. He called a friend of mine a few months later and told him what had happened.

Amazingly Ya'akov's story has a happy ending. After rejecting the faith, then abandoning the orthodox lifestyle, he lived in confusion for many years. Recently, however, he has been supernaturally drawn by the Lord, and is being discipled by some folks at Jews for Jesus. I believe that he has a Messianic Jewish wife as well!

Schochet wanted to kidnap me, too—for my own good, of course. Forget the fact that I was nineteen-years-old, an adult and that it would have been illegal. They were motivated by *higher ideals*—they needed to deprogram me. The funny thing about all this was that according to Schochet and people like him, I had been brainwashed!

Had Bryan kidnapped me? *No!*

Had Dean held a gun to my head and forced me to endure the movie about Yeshua? *No!*

After the wreck, did that fine couple in North Carolina lock me in their basement and say, "Believe in Jesus or we will never let you out"? *No!*

My question here is, *"Who is doing the brainwashing?"* Contrary to their methods, I had received Yeshua of my own free will, after careful consideration and supernatural confirmations.

And yet, Schochet wanted to kidnap me and deprogram me, which I know from first-hand accounts, would have included being held somewhere *against my will*, possibly being drugged, and having his ideology forced down my throat until I denied the Messiah. That, my friend, is brainwashing!

My parents told him *no*—there would be no kidnapping. However, they did ask me to go hear Schochet *the Butcher* at the Jewish Community Center. Ironically *Schochet* is Hebrew for *butcher,* and quite an apt description for him considering that, in addition to slaughtering the souls he came into contact with by any and all means, he would also intentionally *butcher* the Scriptures knowing that none of his listeners was familiar with the New Covenant. He took whole passages completely out of context, aware that no one would know any better. To give just one example, he told the following story from the New Testament to show *how cruel and unloving Yeshua was.*

> A Canaanite woman from that vicinity came to him, crying out, "Lord, Son of David, have mercy on me! My daughter is suffering terribly from demon possession." Jesus did not answer a word. So his disciples came to him and urged him, "Send her away, for she keeps crying out after us." He answered, "I was sent only to the lost sheep of Israel." The woman came and knelt before him. "Lord, help me!" she said. He replied, "It is not right to take the children's bread and toss it to the dogs." (Matthew 15:22-26)

If you stop there, as Rabbi Schochet did on that occasion, it makes Yeshua appear quite callous. However, the story doesn't end there and if you kept reading, you would see that Yeshua was merely testing her faith.

> "Yes, Lord," she said, "but even the dogs eat the crumbs
> that fall from their master's table." Then Jesus answered,
> *"Woman, you have great faith! Your request is granted."*
> *And her daughter was healed from that very hour.* (Matthew
> 15:27-28)

Out of respect and consideration for my parents who were sitting right beside me, I resisted the impulse to stand up and publicly request that he keep reading. It took a lot of self-control to remain silent as he deliberately twisted the truth.

After the meeting, I met with Rabbi Schochet and three other rabbis at Rabbi Kranz's house from 10 p.m. until 2 a.m. Bob Smith came with me. Schochet was sharp. He had me spinning in circles in no time. And let's be honest, as much as I respected Bob as a mentor, he was no match for a Talmudic scholar. Bob was a contractor who could teach and preach the Word with clarity and anointing—but debating a skilled deprogrammer was another thing altogether.

And yet Bob surprised me by getting right to the heart of the matter—albeit after four hours of the rabbi ripping me to shreds. Bob finally stepped in.

"Rabbi Schochet, tonight at the Jewish Community Center during your lecture, when the young lady asked you how to know God, you told her *to study. Study the Torah and the Talmud.* Let me ask you something. Do you love your wife with your head or with your heart?" The rabbi thought for a moment, looked around at the other rabbis, and then burst into laughter. He never answered the question… but he didn't have to.

*Go, Bob!*

Bob's point was very simple. You don't spend time with your wife for knowledge, but intimacy, friendship and companionship. In the same way, the girl was not asking the rabbi for information about God, but for the way to a real, intimate relationship with Him. But sadly, the rabbi could not give what he did not possess.

Rabbi Schochet undoubtedly had great intellectual knowledge, but he did not have a personal, experiential relationship with the living God. As Saul of Tarsus, the rabbi who penned most of the New Covenant, said, "For I can testify about [religious Jews] that they are zealous for God, but their zeal is not based on knowledge... For it is with your *heart* you believe and are justified" (Rom. 10:2, 10a).

Despite Bob's lack of scholarly training, he *knew* God and stumped the *Butcher*.

## RELIGION VS. RELATIONSHIP

Aside from theological disagreements, this really is the primary difference between Messianic Judaism and Modern Rabbinic Judaism: this issue of relationship. In Yeshua, I have met God. It's not a case of merely reading *about* Him, or of observing traditions that are remotely *connected to* Him—but actually *knowing* Him!

Messianic Jews enjoy the presence of God, whereas Orthodox Jews have a religion of *things they must do*. Many of those things are beautiful and meaningful; many, however, are tedious and rote. But all they accomplish, and this is true of religion in general, from Islam to Catholicism, is to make the observer of these traditions and codes of behavior feel good about himself or herself.

They mistake the self-satisfaction and pride, which come from keeping a list of rules, for God's approval. Most religions focus on *what you must do*, not realizing that there is, in fact, *nothing you can do* to earn God's forgiveness—we are all sinners. Salvation is a free gift God offers each one of us through Yeshua alone.

> For the wages of sin is death, but the (FREE) *gift of God* is eternal life through Yeshua, our Messiah and Lord. (Rom. 6:23)

## BIBLE HEROES AND GOD

We do not see the great men such as Abraham, Moses, Joshua, or King David consumed with traditions and ordinances, do we? They were consumed with God Himself. Abraham was called *the friend of God* (Isaiah 41:8, 2 Chronicles 20:7) and Moses pleaded with God for His presence.

> Then Moses said to him, "If your Presence does not go with us, do not send us up from here..." And the LORD said to Moses, "I will do the very thing you have asked, because I am pleased with you and I know you by name." Then Moses said, "Now show me your glory." (Ex. 33:17-18)

We read in Joshua over and over again: "And the Lord said to Joshua..." Joshua communed with God. Of King David, it was said, "He was a man after God's own heart" (1 Samuel 13:14). His passion was not endless rote tradition, but *God himself.* Psalm 27 states it beautifully as David cries out to the Lord:

> One thing I ask from the LORD,
>     this only do I seek:
> that I may dwell in the house of the LORD
>     all the days of my life,

to gaze on the beauty of the L ORD
and to seek him in his temple. (Ps. 27:45)

## MODERN JUDAISM VS. BIBLE JUDAISM

How very different modern-day Rabbinic Judaism is from
the Judaism of the Bible! Modern-day Judaism cannot give you
a relationship with God; it can only give you information about
Him and a list of *mitzvot* (good deeds) to perform.

Ask your rabbi if he has the presence of God in his life. Ask
him if he has a living, personal relationship with God.

## MOSES (LAW) AND YEHOSHUA (GOD IS SALVATION)

Rabbinic Judaism emphasizes the Law—Moses. In fact,
the word Moses is synonymous with the Torah. Could it be that
the fact that Moses could not lead the children of Israel into the
Promised Land was God saying that the Law cannot save you?
Yes, I know Moses was punished for striking the rock twice, but
still, was God seeking to communicate a powerful truth?

How amazing that the one who did lead them across the
Jordan River into the Promised Land was named Yehoshua
(Joshua), which is the long form of Jesus' Hebrew name, Yeshua.
Moses (the Law) could only see the Promised Land, but Yehoshua,
(which means *God is Salvation*) was to possess it.

## IS THE TORAH BAD?

To be clear, *the Torah is not bad* (Rom. 7:12), it just can't
produce life (Gal. 3:21). It can point to life (Gal. 3:24), just as Moses
was able to climb Mount Nebo and see the Promised Land.

135

> Therefore, you (Moses) will see the land only from a
> distance; you will not enter the land I am giving to the
> people of Israel. (Deut. 32:52)

But what the Law could not do, the sacrifice of Yeshua has accomplished. Through the New Covenant (Brit Hadashah) He made a way for you to individually enter into a vibrant, powerful relationship with God Himself. Through Moses God is revealed—you can see Him; through Yeshua, you can know Him.

The Law points to righteousness, but stops short of being able to change you; Yeshua, however, empowers you with righteousness and enables you to live a new life. Just as the Prophet Ezekiel predicted concerning the Jewish people in the end times.

> I will sprinkle clean water on you, and you will be clean;
> I will cleanse you from all your impurities and from
> all your idols. I will give you a new heart and put a
> new spirit in you; I will remove from you your heart of
> stone and give you a heart of flesh. And I will put my
> Spirit in you and move you to follow my decrees and be
> careful to keep my laws. (Ez. 36:25-27)

Jeremiah said that this will be the mark of the New Covenant, the feature that differentiates it from the Old Covenant—that the Torah would not be merely something read on tablets of stone, but on the hearts of men.

> "This is the covenant I will make with the people of
> Israel after that time," declares the LORD.
> "*I will put my law in their minds*
>    and *write it on their hearts.*
> I will be their God,
>    and they will be my people." (Jer. 31:31)

The main point: God isn't looking for people to simply follow rules and tradition, but to know Him. Do you want to know Him? Or is mere religion enough for you?

## AFTERMATH!

Despite Bob's ability to get to the heart of the matter, I still left Rabbi Kranz's house that evening, feeling very confused. In my heart, I was absolutely sure that Yeshua was the Messiah. *I knew Him.* He had become my companion and had set me free from sins I could not have gotten free from on my own. Yet Schochet was a man skilled in his vocation; he knew what he was doing. He knew exactly what to do to fill my head with doubt. I offered a quick but desperate prayer to the Lord before I turned the key in the ignition, "Yeshua, I know You are the Messiah, but could You prove it to me just one more time?"

## A QUICK ANSWER

The phone was ringing. *What time is it?* I wondered. I didn't realize how late I'd slept. I hadn't got to bed until 3:00 a.m. due to the mega-meeting with the rabbis.

"Hello," I said in a voice that signified that I had just woken up. "Hello, Ron, this is Betty Koukle from *Jews for Jesus*. I heard that you had become a believer and I wanted to call and let you know that you are not alone. There are many Jews who believe..." Immediately, I remembered my prayer from the night before. *Father, was this the answer?*

A few days later I saw my friend Scott Brindley. "Hey Ron, did Betty Koukle call you the other day?"

"Yes, she did. Why do you ask?" I answered

"Oh, it's just that she called me on Tuesday morning asking for your number. She said *the Lord had told her to call you that morning.*"

THE LORD HAD TOLD HER TO CALL ME!!!

"Yes, God, it *was* you! Thank you Father!"

Some of you may be thinking, what do you mean *the Lord TOLD her to call you? Is she Moses, hearing such voices?* One of the wonderful things about knowing Yeshua is the personal relationship you enjoy with Him. He does *speak* to us. Mostly it is not an audible voice, but an inner sense.

You might want to ask your rabbi *if God speaks to him.* You may think we are just hearing voices in our heads, but I can give you scores of documented testimonies where, what people heard the Lord say, proved to be correct or came to pass. Always God's word to His children is relevant, timely, and directive, providing exactly what is needed in the situation.

# CHAPTER TWENTY

## JEWISH BROOKLYN—KIPPAS IN THE PIZZA PARLOR

My encounter with Rabbi Schochet and company would not be my last meeting with rabbis who tried to discredit my faith. A year later my mother and I were having a conversation about Yeshua. "If you can find a Jewish person who *knows* God, I will meet with him," I challenged her.

As I said earlier, modern-day Judaism does not profess to bring you into a relationship with God. Whenever I met a rabbi, I would ask him, "Do you *know* God?" Most would say something like, "You can't really know God, but you can know *about* Him." I always answered honestly, "Well, I know God; until you can offer me as much, I am not interested!"

I have a personal, intimate relationship with Yeshua. I feel His presence. I see evidence of Him in my life. Why would I want to trade that for *religion*?

My mother took me seriously and found Rabbi Yehuda Fine in Brooklyn. *Brooklyn!* I could have picked up the phone and called fifty people in Richmond who claimed they knew God, but *the closest* traditional Jewish person my mother could find was five hundred miles north! At the time I was unaware that he was also *a trained expert in working with Messianic Jews.*

It was at this time that I was introduced to Dr. Michael Brown. Dr. Brown is a Messianic Jew and was at that time a Bible College Professor on Long Island. Today he is arguably the foremost Messianic apologist in the world. (An apologist is someone who offers convincing arguments in defense of something controversial.) Dr. Brown's series of books, *Answering Jewish Objections to Jesus,* is perhaps the most exhaustive work on this subject to date. Bryan had been attending CFNI Bible College on Long Island where Dr. Brown was teaching and put me in touch with his professor. Not only was he Jewish, but he was a Hebrew scholar and had a Ph.D. in ancient Semitic languages. Dr. Brown helped prepare me to withstand the onslaught that would come against me over the next four days of meetings with Yehuda and his assistant, Scott.

I quickly found out why we had to travel five hundred miles to Brooklyn to meet with a Jew who *claimed* to know God. As I mentioned earlier, Yehuda was an Orthodox Jewish psychologist. With Yehuda was Scott, a former Jewish biker turned Orthodox. He served as Yehuda's disciple. Their area of expertise was in dealing with people like me—Jewish young people who had discovered the Jewish Messiah. Their job was to make me feel accepted and to show understanding. However, this was just as manipulative an approach as Schochet's deprogramming tactics. It is interesting that Messianic Jews are accused of using *love-bombing* to lure people into our movement—a clearly cultic practice and something *we do not do.* Yet that is exactly what Scott and Yehuda were trying to do to me.

They asked me to tell them how I came to believe in Yeshua. As I shared with them the story you have just read, I sensed the presence of the Holy Spirit. After I finished, it was clear to me that they had been impacted by my testimony—or at least pretended to have been touched.

"We believe that you have had an encounter with God," Yehuda said.

Wow! That statement deeply encouraged me. It was the first time that a traditional Jew had affirmed the notion that God had anything to do with what had happened to me. I was also glad that they, Orthodox Jews, had said this in front of my parents. As they continued though, I realized there was a catch.

"But Ron, we believe that because you were so *turned off* to traditional Judaism, God used Jesus to get your attention, and now He wants you to come back to Judaism. You see, Jesus is the way for the Gentiles; but Judaism is the way for the Jews."

So, let me get this straight. God has this guy, Yeshua, be born in *Israel*, preach and do miracles among *Jewish* people, and fulfill all the prophecies the Jewish prophets made about the Jewish Messiah[7]—all for the benefit of the Gentiles!?

Yeshua's life parallels the description of the Messiah prophesied by Isaiah in Chapter 53. He dies on Passover and rises from the dead three days later on Firstfruits. Then God births the Messianic movement on Shavuot, the Feast of Weeks, and all this takes place in *Jerusalem*! His *Jewish* followers write twenty-seven books[8] (the New Covenant) and go all over *Israel* telling *Jewish* people about their Messiah, Yeshua. This gospel is proclaimed "first to the Jew" (Romans 1:16). These same Jewish followers only reluctantly, after about ten years, start sharing the message of Yeshua with the Gentiles… and you guys are telling me that all this is for the benefit of the *GOYIM* (Gentiles)!!!

If He is the Messiah for anyone *then He is the Messiah for the Jews*. When you see Yeshua in His *original Jewish context*, there is NO possibility that He is the God of the Gentiles only and not the Jews.

Well, I didn't respond like that. I was young. Today I am forty-seven-years-old with a degree in theology and have just

7       That is, the prophecies referring to His first coming.
8       There is much debate on whether or not Luke was Jewish.

spent the last year of my life researching the Jewishness of Jesus and how it has been stolen from Him... so it is very easy to refute and expose the fallacy of their logic now. But, back then I was not prepared for their onslaught.

Scott and Yehuda spoke like believers. They used terminology that I had not heard Jewish people use before. They spoke about God's Word like they read it devotionally. They shared about God as if they knew Him—but they didn't! I now know that it was all an act to make me think that in modern-day Judaism, I could have everything I found in Messianic Judaism. They were conmen, hirelings with a job to do—*destroy my faith!*

To be clear, I think they were *honest conmen,* meaning, they genuinely thought they were helping me. They were not like Schochet *the Butcher*. And to be honest, I liked them. Their lifestyle was attractive. Everything they did was centered on the beautiful traditions of Judaism. The *guilt* factored in as well.

"Ron, you're a Jew! How can you believe in Jesus? You have turned your back on your people, on the Holocaust. Ron, you are a traitor." No, they didn't say it exactly like that, but I sure felt it—not only from them, but also from my fellow Jews everywhere. And I don't blame them. So much horror has been perpetrated against Jews in the name of Jesus. Even Hitler claimed to be God's servant, finishing what the Church had begun.

And who enjoys being labeled a fanatic—an outcast? I truly wanted to be accepted by my fellow Jews. By the end of our time together, I thought, *Maybe they are right? Maybe God is using Jesus to bring me back to Judaism? Maybe I can have everything I have found in Yeshua, without Him?* They certainly succeeded in instilling some confusion in my mind.

But how could I deny the existence of my best Friend? He *was* real. Not only because the Hebrew Scriptures proved it, but also because I'd met Him, I knew Him! Nevertheless, there was doubt.

On the last day of our trip, Scott and I went to a local pizza parlor. In this part of Brooklyn, everyone and everything is Jewish. It was so strange to see the guys making pizzas wearing *kippot* (head coverings). It was also attractive to me. I wanted this lifestyle. Their plan was beginning to work. I fantasized about leaving the faith and becoming an Orthodox Jew. No one would reject me and I could be religious. How funny it was that I was now thinking like this, considering how much I had hated religion before. I was obviously very confused.

I took a walk through the streets of Manhattan shortly before we left the hotel for the airport. "Lord, I know You are the truth. I have a relationship with You. Nothing can replace You in my life. Nobody could have changed me like You have!"

Although I was sure of my relationship with God, my desire for acceptance and my longing for things Jewish were influencing me. Jewish Brooklyn was looking very attractive. I could envision myself moving to such a place and living as they did. Indeed, many have denied the faith to fully embrace the traditions of Judaism, unwilling to endure alienation from the community. The order of Shabbat, the shutting down of all businesses and meeting with the men to pray three times a day—it had its draw. What would I do?

I asked Yeshua to prove himself to me one more time.

It was Saturday night, and I had arrived back in Richmond on the Friday. Friends of mine were hosting a Bible study at the University of Richmond. A local pastor named Carpenter was to be the guest speaker. Now I had never met Pastor Carpenter, and he had no way of knowing where I had just been. But that night he called me out of the gathering and told me that God wanted to say something to me.

"Son, I have seen what you have just been through. It was a test, and you have passed the test. You did not give in to the pressure but remained true."

I couldn't believe my ears. Jimmy, Gary, and some of my other friends began to laugh, recognizing that this was supernatural. Once again, God had moved to strengthen and restore my wavering faith.

Of course, that was just one of the many loving and timely words of encouragement I would receive over the years from the God who had once been so far away, but now had become so very close. It is not, however, the basis for my faith. I have studied the Scriptures diligently, sought God with all my heart, discussed the issues with intelligent rabbis, and seen the Lord's faithful hand over and over again. I *know* the certainty of what I believe. My faith rests on the written Word of the Hebrew Scriptures, but God's supernatural intervention in my life is always very welcome!

# CHAPTER TWENTY-ONE

## OFF TO COLLEGE... AGAIN

I decided to attend the Bible College where Dr. Michael Brown served as Academic Dean. I was apprehensive because this was my first real attempt at school as a believer. In many ways it was my first real attempt at school. I did not want to leave there with a 1.7 GPA as I did from high school. Remember, I had only read one book cover to cover by the time I became a believer. Now I was going to seek a degree in Theology. How would I sit still? How would I focus? And homework? Where would I find the motivation to do homework?

Fortunately, my time at CFNI was quite the opposite of my time at Mils E. Godwin High School. I graduated with a 3.85 GPA and have the transcripts to prove it. Was this the same guy who cheated on tests, never studied, and got friends to write papers for him? You may be thinking that Bible college was just easier. Not so. When Dr. Brown gave us our final exam on *Job and the God of the Old Testament*, I was one of only four people to pass. The rest of the class failed. I received a score of 102 percent. I don't say that to put my class down or to build myself up, but simply to say that God had truly done a miracle in my life.

One morning in Bible college while I was praying, my thoughts kept being drawn to the youth of Beth Messiah Congregation in Rockville, MD. There was no logical reason why I should have been thinking about this particular youth group. I didn't know any of the kids in the group and had only visited that congregation twice in two years. Yet, strangely, when I finished praying that morning I just knew that I would soon be the youth leader there.

That very same day, Dr. Brown's wife, Nancy, came up to me and said, "Beth Messiah's youth group needs you." I was stunned! Nancy had no idea what the Lord had told me that morning. Then a few months later during a time of prayer, the Lord put it in my heart that I was to move to Maryland after I graduated from Bible college. Within one month of my move to Maryland, Eitan Shishkoff, the senior leader of Beth Messiah Congregation, came and asked me to become their youth leader.

## HEAVEN-SENT WHEELS

A month before I moved to Maryland I didn't have a car, a job, or a place to live. I was living in Richmond over the summer working for my father while preparing to move. On my way to work one day, I looked out the window and saw a Honda Accord and a Honda Prelude. Suddenly I heard an inner voice asking, "Which one do you want?"

"The Prelude of course," I answered. It was sportier than the Accord. But as I thought about it, wisdom got the better of me and I changed my mind and said, "Lord, the Prelude isn't very practical. I need more space. I'll take the Accord."

Believing in Yeshua doesn't guarantee us new cars and material possessions. Yet, here I was at twenty-one, willing to follow God wherever He would lead me (on foot if necessary), and He was offering me a Honda Accord. To be honest, my plan had been to buy a ten-speed and bike all over Rockville, Maryland!

Then, a short time later, I was riding home from work with my father, when he unexpectedly said, "Ron, I have decided to give you Michele's car."

My father could not figure out why I was not excited at the prospect of getting my sister's old car. He was going to buy her a new one. Even though he swore he would never help me as long as I continued to pursue a life in ministry, he'd now relented to the extent that he was going to let me have her old car. (If I remember correctly, we were on our way home from the bike store and the thought of his son using a bicycle as his primary mode of transport may have had something to do with his change of heart.)

It wasn't that I wasn't grateful. I was extremely grateful, but God had told me He was going to give me a Honda Accord. "Thanks, Dad." I did not dare tell him about the Accord.

A few days later, my father called and said he was bringing home a car for my sister.

"What kind of car is it, Dad?" I asked.

"A Honda," he said.

Gulp! "Dad, is it a Honda *Accord*?"

"Yes, Ron. Why?"

"Oh, I was just wondering…"

Was this really happening? *Was this my car, and my Dad just didn't know it yet?* I called my friend Jimmy. I had told him a month before that God was going to give me a Honda Accord. Jimmy said that even if I did not get the car, the fact that my sister was getting an Accord was proof enough for him that God had spoken.

Well, my sister took one look at the car and didn't like it. My father could return it to Joe Woodfin, a local used car dealer with whom we had been doing business for years. He was more than a used car dealer; my dad had other business with him. When we needed a new car, Joe would find it. If we didn't like it, he'd just sell it to someone else. So Michele not liking the car simply meant that my father would return it to Joe. However, this was not going back to Joe. This was my car!

In my impatience, I figured I would help God out a bit.

"I'll take it, Dad!" I said.

"No. Absolutely not!" He continued to make it abundantly clear that under no circumstances was he going to give me that car. It was one thing to give me Michele's old Dodge which was already paid for and had close to 100,000 miles on the odometer, but he was certainly not going to send me to Maryland in a late model Honda Accord. Dejected, I turned and walked out of the room to get my laundry out of the dryer. As I did, it was as if the Lord spoke and said, "Are you done? Now, watch Me work!" My heart was flooded with peace and I knew God was in control. On the other hand, my dad's words were so adamant that it seemed impossible that he would ever give me the car.

Five minutes later I heard my father yell my name from the porch. From the tone of his voice I thought he was mad at me. As I walked out onto the porch, the keys to the Honda Accord came flying across the room. "It's yours," he said.

# CHAPTER TWENTY-TWO

## ELANA VAKNIN

Just before I finished Bible college, I told a friend that I was going to move to Maryland, meet my wife, and marry her next August. And, believe it or not, it happened just that way.

Now, I would love to tell you the story of how I met and married my wife, Elana Vaknin, an Israeli believer from Ashkelon, a small city south of Tel Aviv... but I'm going to let her tell you instead.


*Here is her story in her own words:*

Three years after my parents emigrated from Casablanca, Morocco to Israel, I was born in Jerusalem. We were a traditional Sephardic Jewish Family (meaning we came from a Middle Eastern or Mediterranean nation).

In our Holy City of Jerusalem, the men in our family continued to go to synagogue on Friday evenings and during the day the women cooked a festive meal. Until today, my mother is still an amazing cook. When she comes to visit us in Ra'anana (just north of Tel Aviv), within minutes our home is filled with delicious smells of cumin, garlic and other Mediterranean spices.

I always believed that God was real. When our family prayed on Yom Kippur, many of my Israeli friends fasted out of guilt or duty, but I truly believed that God was listening. Even though I knew He was real, I didn't have a deep connection with Him—I didn't know that such a thing as a relationship with God, was possible.

The early decades of our brand new country were exhilarating. We were building a nation! I had no time for drugs, alcohol or cigarettes. My greatest passion as a teenager was my involvement in the *Tsofim* (Scouts). Now, the Scouts in Israel cannot be compared to the Scouts in the U.S. Every kid in Israel joined the Scouts and we all knew that much of what we learned there would help us once we joined the army, as every Israeli (except the Ultra-Orthodox) is required to do.

The course was very comprehensive and sometimes quite demanding. We would navigate by the stars and sleep in the desert. We would hike for miles and miles on the Golan Heights, around the Sea of Galilee, and in the Negev Desert. In addition, we would help out at nursing homes and a range of other public institutions. During Passover and in the summer we would serve as guides to younger Scouts. The focus of Scouts was on *serving our country*—our precious, young country.

My other great love was the beach. As I was approaching my teen years, we moved to Ashkelon on the coast. This brand new city built on the sand dunes that grace the Mediterranean coast is an hour south of Tel Aviv and just a few minutes north of Gaza. I could walk to the beach – and I did, often!

You might be thinking that being so close to Gaza was dangerous, but back then we got along well with the Arabs who lived there. My father would take me shopping for vegetables in Gaza and I felt perfectly safe. However, once the PLO infiltrated the people of Gaza, they turned against us, sadly, ruining their economy. While Arafat got rich, the poor Arabs of Gaza suffered increasing poverty.

I graduated from high school in 1983 and volunteered to serve the nation through a special, six month long program in the Scouts. We went to a small pioneering kibbutz (a collective community traditionally based on agriculture) with a few families who were just starting out. We cultivated the new vegetable gardens, picked cotton and when ripe, picked the fruit from the trees. I loved being outside, working with my hands and watching our nation grow.

## SERVING IN THE AIR FORCE

After my season on the kibbutz, it was time to enter the Israeli Defense Forces (IDF) where I served in the Air Force as a drill sergeant for pilots. In Israel, pilots are highly revered. So, as a young lady, I felt myself very lucky to be surrounded by so many handsome pilots!

After my two years of IDF service I started college at Wingate Institute for Physical Education, named after a famous British Major General and Christian Zionist who helped train Jewish soldiers before Israel was even a state. While many of the British soldiers were helping the Arabs, he felt it was his religious duty to help Israel become a nation. To this day Orde Wingate is referred to as *The Friend* here in Israel.

I studied physical education and met Dalit, my best friend there. Her family had escaped the Soviet Union long before Perestroika and Glasnost, during a brief window of opportunity in 1971 when a number of Jewish families were permitted to leave Russia. She was my roommate at Wingate and even today, lives just twenty minutes away from me. We did everything together, including going to America.

## OFF TO AMERICA

It is traditional for Israeli youth to travel abroad after they finish their army service or college. Some hike in South America, or travel as far afield as Australia and New Zealand, while others go to India or Thailand to do drugs. Me, I wanted to go to America—to see Hollywood, New York, Las Vegas and the Grand Canyon.

Dalit's family lived in Oregon, so we decided we would head there after taking a brief bite out of the *Big Apple*. From Oregon we would then continue our trip around the United States. On the airplane ride over the Atlantic, Dalit turned to me and told me that there was something that she needed to tell me. She started out by saying, ***"I believe that Yeshua is the Messiah of the Jewish people."***

At the time Dalit was not walking with the Lord, but she knew I was going meet her family in a few weeks—especially, her mother, who was anything but shy about sharing her faith. Dalit was preparing me.

Our first stop was New York where we met her cousin and his wife. We stayed there with them for a couple of weeks. They were so sweet and I found out that they, too, believed in Yeshua. Before we left to continue our trip, they told me, "We have a present for you." It was a Hebrew New Testament.

While many Jews might have been hesitant to receive such a book, the truth is, I didn't even fully understand what it was. Unlike Ron, I did not grow up surrounded by Christian culture. In Israel there is no Christmas or Easter—at least not in Ashkelon. I knew very little about anything outside of Israel. While we did have some American television shows, it was nothing like today, where most Israeli youth can speak English *because* of TV.

152

## GOD PURSUED ME!

I began to read it as we traveled. It didn't really make much sense to me, yet I now know that God was clearly trying to get my attention. Our next stop was Los Angeles and we were already down to our last pennies. So, as Israeli youth do when they travel, we went looking for jobs in a restaurant, hoping to wash dishes for a few weeks until we had enough money to move on to our next stop.

Suddenly a man came up to us on a bus and said, "Are you from Israel? God told me to give you this." In his hand was $20. I was truly dumbfounded. I had never heard anybody speak like that. *God told him?!!!*

Along the way, Dalit remembered a woman called Paula, whom she'd once met at a Messianic conference in Israel. Paula then invited us to her home and we stayed with her for a week. This woman loved Israel so much! She was part of a home group that prayed for the Jewish people every single day.

She loved on me and I was drawn to her faith. She was, without my realizing it, fulfilling the Scripture that says that salvation has come to the Gentiles to make Israel jealous (Romans 11:11).

I wanted what she had, even though I didn't really know what it was. She was just one of many believers I met as we traveled and they were all so kind to me. Through Paula, we made connections with other believers.

In San Francisco we were invited to attend a concert—by a Christian singer named Michael Card.

After the concert we were introduced to him. He was excited to learn that I was from Israel and gave me one of his CDs. I loved his music; it touched me deeply.

All of these events and people were divinely planned. Each one touched my life and opened my heart a little bit more to want to know God.

## SALVATION COMES

Toward the end of that year, we attended a large conference in Washington, D.C. for Messianic Jews. That night a man by the name of Dr. Michael Brown brought a powerful message. His assistant was a young man named Ron Cantor. I didn't actually meet Ron at the conference, but who could have known that my husband to be was there at that meeting before I was even a believer? At the end of the message people were literally crying as they repented.

I had never seen anything like this before and, quite honestly, I thought they were all crazy. I just wanted to get out of that place. I tried, frantically, to get out of my seat, but I couldn't move! It was as if I was glued to my chair.

Then I heard a voice inside me. "Close your eyes and you will know that I am real." As I did, I felt warm oil being poured out all over me and then I started to weep. I didn't fully understand what was happening, but I knew that this was from my God, the God of Israel. At the same moment, Dalit returned with all her heart to her Messiah!

Later that evening I met with a Messianic leader and Holocaust survivor, Eliezer Urbach. He explained to me more about Yeshua and prayed with me to receive salvation and eternal life. After that I was so hungry for God! I wanted to go to Bible studies and to know Yeshua more deeply. While working at odd jobs, Dalit and I were taken in by a woman named Joanne who attended Beth Messiah, a Messianic Congregation in Rockville, Maryland.

We also began to travel a little with the popular Messianic band, *Israel's Hope* with singer, Paul Wilbur. I, along with six other dancers, would perform Israeli folk dances during their concerts. *Life was great.*

## AN URGENT CALL TO COME HOME

Then, just a few months after coming to faith, I received a phone call from my brother in Israel, telling me that my father was sick and that I needed to come home. When I arrived back in Israel, I found the situation was far more serious than I'd been told. He was in a coma as a result of a heart attack.

I loved my father very much. He was such a warm human being and so friendly. In fact, everybody loved Abraham Vaknin. For two weeks I sat by his side, holding his hand, praying earnestly for his salvation.

You know how new believers are! They are so full of their newfound faith! Even though my father could not respond or speak to me, I talked to him continually of our Jewish Messiah, Yeshua. Suddenly, he opened his eyes—*for the first time in two weeks*—looked straight at me and then passed into eternity.

It is my belief that when he opened his eyes and looked at me, it was a sign from God that my father had heard all that I'd said and prayed, and that he had received salvation. Who knows what Heavenly business took place during those two weeks he was in a coma?

After his death I entered into a time of dark depression. I missed him so much. I would go down to the beach every day and cry. The more I thought about it, the more I felt I needed to go back to the U.S. to get stronger in the Lord. I was a new believer and there were so few Israeli believers to turn to at that time—in fact, none that I knew of in Ashkelon.

To tell the truth, I didn't know a single Jewish believer in all of Israel.

## REQUEST FOR U.S. VISA REJECTED

I tried to get a visa to return to America but the American consulate kept refusing me. I was single, without a job and female—a red light to any American consulate agent reviewing a visa application. In addition, the more times you apply for a visa, the less likely you are to get one because each rejection goes on your record.

Yet I wondered why God, Who is so powerful, didn't answer my prayer. On my last try, I desperately prayed, "God, if Yeshua is really my Messiah, please let me get a visa today." That day they granted me a visa and I knew this was God's will for me.

I returned to America and as soon as I arrived some believers got around me and prayed for me. Immediately the heavy black clouds I had been under lifted from me; I was free of depression. I felt again like I did when I first came to faith.

I found work in an Israeli Deli, studied English at Georgetown University, became active in the congregation and began to grow in my faith. Just a few days after I returned, I was introduced to a young man named Ron Cantor—the young man who'd been present the night I came to Yeshua. He was a Jewish believer, a youth leader, and on fire for God. I began to have dreams that we were going to get married!

One evening I sense that the Lord told me during a service that my husband was up in the balcony. I turned around but there was no one at all sitting in the balcony. I thought my mind was playing tricks on me. However, again, I felt a voice inside say, "Turn around. Your husband is in the balcony." When I turned around the second time, Ron was getting up off his knees. He had been up there praying by himself.

Ron was not aware of any of this. But one evening, Ari Sorko Ram, an Israeli Messianic leader was visiting from Israel and he spoke at our singles' group. Ron said that when he walked in and saw me, he just knew that I would be his wife.

Later, Ron took me to meet his parents and his father told him afterward, "Ron, you have to marry that girl. I know she believes in Jesus but at least she is Jewish." Ron received his father's blessing and we were married the following August.

## MAY I CUT IN?

Okay, I need jump in here and tell my side of the story...

From the time Elana landed back in America, Dalit did not stop trying to get the two of us together. As I mentioned earlier, I had just become the youth leader at Beth Messiah and I really wanted to get married, but didn't want to make a mistake.

So when Dalit continued to try and match me up with Elana, I would balk. However, on the night previously mentioned, when Ari Sorko-Ram was speaking at our singles' group, something happened. Elana walked into the room and I was dumbstruck! She was beautiful. Not just gorgeous, but so cute and animated. I began to warm to the idea of getting to know this Israeli girl a little better. I don't know why I didn't see it before—that the wife God was giving me was not only beautiful, not only Jewish, but an Israeli as well!

A few days later, Dalit asked if we could go over to Elana's house. She was living with and working as a nanny for Paul and Luanne Wilbur. Paul has since become one of the most well-known Messianic worship leaders in the world. Dalit was really surprised when this time I said yes. That night we watched *An*

*American Tail (Fieval Mousekewitz)* together and I just sat and stared at my future wife. That night I went home and prayed. It was very late and I was still outside. I said, "Lord, you know I don't want to make a mistake here. I want to be a good example to these youth. I need to know *now*. Is she the one for me?"

"Turn around and you will know," came the answer. I did and noticed that the road I was walking on had merged together with another to become one road. "Your two roads are intersecting and will become one road." Of course I had heard these voices before when it came to future wives, so, knowing myself, I proceeded with caution.

About a week later, I was taking Asher Intrater, a friend and mentor, to a meeting. I was living with Asher and his family at the time and he needed a ride. When we passed a bus stop, Elana was standing there in the freezing cold as the snow came down. I beeped and waved, realizing that I could not stop because I had to drop off Asher. Of course, in her mind, I had just left her out in the cold. Not good.

I dropped Asher off and made a beeline back to the bus stop. *Whew!* She was still there. I took her to school and enjoyed being with my future wife. A few weeks later we began to officially date.

A few weeks later I took Elana to meet my parents, as she has already described. It was a cold wintry day. Thousands of Jewish people had converged on Washington, DC, participating in a march for the release of Soviet Jews. My parents were at the march with a group of their friends. Of course, my parents marched in style—booking a suite at the famed Mayflower Hotel on K Street—the very same hotel where we would spend our honeymoon nine months later. We enjoyed a great breakfast there as I showed off my Messianic Jewish, Israeli girlfriend to all my parents' friends—who were also staying at the Mayflower.

Everyone there fell in love with Elana. And for those of you who know my wife, you can understand why.

What a special day that was. I still remember being with Elana at Chi Chi's Mexican restaurant on Rockville Pike after a long, cold, and exhausting day. What a joy it was to be with God's choice for my life.

Several months later I pulled up in front of her home to drop her off and I said, *"Tinasi li?"* which is Hebrew for "Will you marry me?" She said "Yes!"

And on August 27th 1988, Elana Vaknin became Elana Cantor.


## BABIES!

Several weeks after our wedding, Elana began to have cramps. We were in Richmond when this began. The next day my mother and I took her to the emergency room. Dr. Rabhan examined her and took blood for a pregnancy test. When the blood test came back he said, "It's positive!"

"Oh thank you Lord! We're going to have a baby!" I exclaimed.

"Oh, I am sorry, it's negative," Dr. Rabhan said, correcting himself.

"Oh, thank you Lord! We're not ready for children!" I said.

"No, no, it's positive," said the doctor.

"Huh?" After going back and forth five times, he finally got it right. Elana was pregnant! That was the good news. The bad news was that he was quite sure it was a tubal pregnancy. In the case of a tubal pregnancy, the only thing they can do is to remove the baby. If the baby grows in the fallopian tube, the tube will burst and kill the mother and the child.

He said that he wanted to do an ultrasound before he removed the baby, just to be sure. At that point I left Elana with my mother and went outside the hospital. For the next twenty minutes, I cried out to God. "Father, You are the Author of life, not death! Please get that baby into the uterus!"

After about twenty minutes, a peace came over me. I went back inside just as they were wheeling Elana into the ultrasound room. When they checked her, sure enough, there was Sharon, tiny as she was, in Elana's uterus. Dr. Rabhan looked at me and said, *"I guess my textbooks lied!"*

Exactly nine months and three days after our wedding our first daughter, Sharon Rachel was born. Since then, Yael Hannah and Danielle Rebecca have been added to the family to make *shalosh banot*, three daughters!

# CHAPTER TWENTY-THREE

## HOLDING ON TO A PROMISE

Imentioned in the beginning of the book how my dad and I have a great relationship today. We went from no real relationship before I believed in Yeshua, to a horrible relationship afterward. As a new believer, I was not very sensitive to my parents' feelings. I had no understanding of how difficult it was for them to deal with the fact that their son believed in Jesus. I was very zealous for Yeshua, but not very sympathetic to the problems my faith had created for my parents.

Several years later, I went back to them to ask for their forgiveness. They graciously forgave me and even gave me their blessing to be in the ministry, though they would have preferred that I be in business. To me, this meant a great deal. But that was not the beginning of God's work of restoration in my family. Many years earlier, God had begun to heal my relationship with my father.

When I left for Bible college, my dad and I hardly spoke to each other. I would call home from school, and it was like talking to someone I hardly knew. Many times when I hung up the phone I wanted to cry.

I was holding on to a promise the Lord had made to me. A few years before, Yehuda (the family therapist rabbi from Brooklyn) had offered his services to my father and me, to help us work on our relationship. His main work was not dealing with Jewish teens who had become Messianic, but he is an expert working with problem teens and families. As I said before, I genuinely liked him. I deeply wanted a better relationship with my father but despite my fondness for Yehuda as a person, I did not trust him when it came to my beliefs. It would always be his goal to destroy my faith in Yeshua, even if he would help us in our relationship.

As I prayed about it I sensed that the Lord was telling me that He Himself would restore my relationship with my father. My job was to keep reaching out. While I was at Bible college I wondered if God had really spoken this to me because things only got worse.

However, two years later, after I graduated from CFNI, God began to work on our relationship. The healing started when my father and I took a business trip together to Florida. We had a great time. He had bought the stock of a bankrupt shoe store. He left me at the store to supervise the loading of a truck by some men we'd hired for the day. However, they left before the job was finished! The truck driver and I had to finish loading the shoes into the truck. It was 103 degrees outside and by the time I left, I could hardly move. I missed my plane and went to the hotel and collapsed. Despite the fact that I could barely move a muscle, it was a tremendous feeling to have worked together with my dad.

That was the beginning of the wonderful restoration that God did in our relationship. Today I consider my dad one of my best friends. There are few people I would rather be with than my father. Both of my parents have been very generous to Elana and me over the years. When we were first married, and broke, they helped us. They also helped us to buy our first home. I am very grateful for my parents. I was so rotten to them as a child, and they have been so wonderful to me. My prayer now is for the rest of my family *to see their need for Yeshua and give their lives to Him.*

## COUSIN BECKY AND AUNT MYRA

While on the subject of family, I have two wonderful stories I would like to share with you. I meet believers all the time who have a long history of faith in their family line. Their parents are believers, their cousins, aunts and uncles are believers—even their dog has, on occasion, been caught saying grace before a meal. However, for most of us Jewish believers, we are alone. When I embraced Yeshua, I didn't have one person in my extended family tree, that I knew of, who was a believer.

Back in the late nineties, however, I was in for a great surprise. I was speaking at the Shabbat service at Tikvat Israel, a Messianic congregation in Richmond, where I grew up. I had no idea that Becky Huff was waking up in Richmond that morning as well. (She lived in Blacksburg, with her husband Chris.) Becky was thinking to herself, *I am Jewish. I have been a believer in Yeshua now for six years but I have never been to a Messianic service. I need to go.* And that same morning she came to Tikvat Israel.

At the end of my message, Becky came up to me and said, "Hi Ron, I am your cousin, Becky!" It was like Scrabble letters in my brain. It didn't make sense—no one in my family believes—and suddenly a seven-letter-word began to form, as it hit me. *I have a relative who believes in Yeshua!* I hadn't seen Becky since we were children, growing up on Cutshaw Avenue, and since she is a few years younger than I am, we'd never been that close.

I can only imagine what she was feeling during that service, as she, too, had thought she was the only believer in her extended family. She had to sit through my entire message feeling like she would explode before she was able to approach me with the good news. Now, she is like a sister to me and her husband Chris is a like a brother.

Second, and this story is somewhat more recent, in late February of 2012, I received an email from my aunt, completely out of the blue. I hadn't seen her in years. She related that for the past six months she had been going to a Baptist church. She said she really wanted to receive Yeshua but she felt guilty, being Jewish. That led to frequent correspondence over the following two weeks. During that time she visited the same congregation mentioned above—Tikvat Israel—and loved it. She realized there that she could be Jewish *and* believe in Yeshua.

So when I got to Richmond, we met for coffee and she prayed to receive Yeshua into her heart!!! HALLELUJAH! Another Cantor in the Kingdom!!! Six months later, as of this writing, she is still going strong and even brought my other aunt and her husband to hear me speak just a few weeks ago. Recently, she went through the *Jewish ritual* of water immersion. Is God up to something in my family? I sure hope so. I know that all those prayers, prayed for all these years, are stored up in Heaven. May this be the time of harvest for my family!

I need to explain here that the building that Tikvat Israel now owns was originally an Orthodox Jewish synagogue—Beth Israel. It was sold to a Baptist church, and then many years later, Tikvat Israel purchased it. My aunt, as well as my father, went to Shul there as children. *Now, as I have just relayed, my aunt has returned there as a Messianic believer!* You can imagine how surprised she was to recognize another woman her age at the congregation, someone she knew from their Beth Israel synagogue days *over fifty years ago!*

My father had also had his Bar Mitzvah in that synagogue. So, since we were living in Richmond and attending Tikvat Israel when our oldest daughter, Sharon, turned thirteen, she celebrated her Bat Mitzvah as a Messianic Jewish young lady, in the very same synagogue where her grandfather had celebrated his! This made it a doubly significant occasion for us all.

The hand of God was so unmistakably behind each of these seemingly chance events. What fun it is to serve the Living God!

# EPILOGUE

Well, the story of course, doesn't end there. We raised our girls in Gaithersburg, MD, where I served not only as the youth leader but also as associate Messianic Rabbi for a number of years at Beth Messiah Congregation. I was privileged to sit under the mentoring of men like Dr. Dan Juster, Dr. Michael Brown, Asher Intrater, Eitan Shishkoff and Jerry Miller.

In 1998 we moved our tribe of five to Odessa, Ukraine to spend a year serving with the Messianic Jewish Bible Institute (MJBI). There was a great move of God amongst the Russian-speaking Jews after the Iron Curtain came down, stirring several ministries to partner together to start a Bible college to train needed leaders for Jewish ministry. Still, this was no small sacrifice for my Israeli wife. On our first visit to Odessa, wild dogs roamed the runway as our plane landed. When we arrived at the apartment of some soon-to-be colleagues, Elana pointed out a dead mouse in the courtyard and thought, *There is no way I am bringing my girls to this place.* However, a divine encounter changed all that.

After the visit, I was feeling very impressed by the Lord that we were to move there. Elana still couldn't bring herself to move our family halfway across the world to what was, in our eyes, a third world nation. One morning she broke down—in a department store of all places! Right there, feeling the weight of it all, she started crying. An older female employee there approached her. "What's the matter? Can I help?"

Elana brushed her off, saying, "No, this is something you wouldn't understand."

The lady persisted and Elana said, "Well, my husband wants to move our family to Ukraine, to teach in a Bible school and I am terrified to take my children there."

The lady warmed to Elana and said, "Oh sweetie, you have nothing to worry about. My husband and I served in Africa as Baptist missionaries for twenty-five years and they were the best years of my life." Elana was stunned. That divine appointment brought a peace to her heart and within six months we were once again greeting the wild dogs on the runway of Odessa's airport.

My girls still recall the excitement and strangeness of living in a country where open-air meat markets displayed the heads of pigs and tongues of cows outside in ninety degree heat, where Mafia controlled the local economy, and where taxis were anyone willing to stop and give you a ride for the price of five *grevna* ($1) each way to school. Local police were not about justice. They were more intent on accusing you of any ridiculous crime they could invent, just so you would bribe them with a beer or bottle of vodka. It was a totally unforgettable season of our lives and to this day, my girls are in touch with some of the young people they met that year.

About halfway through our time there, we were challenged to host a Messianic outreach festival in a city called Berdichev. In May 1999, we, along with the students of the MJBI and many other Messianic Jews in Ukraine, headed to Berdichev. Berdichev is the city upon which the play and movie *Fiddler on the Roof* was based. Shalom Aleichem, the play's author, grew up there.

Valintin Sviontek, Anton Antonovich and I traveled six hours through snow and pothole ridden roads to meet with the leading charismatic pastor and his team. Instantly there was *kesher*—a connection. This pastor not only made his building available to us, he also recommended a Jewish couple to lead the new congregation and, in the early years, helped us to oversee the new work, as we were not local.

After two nights of outreach we birthed the congregation on Shabbat. To this day the Berdichev congregation remains one of the stronger Messianic works in Ukraine under the leadership of Vadim and Fiona Keldish. On Sunday the pastor had me share with his congregation about the spirit of antisemitism. It was the most emotional message I had ever given. More than once I broke down in tears. At one point as I continued, I noticed that there was no interpretation. I looked to see my interpreter overwhelmed and unable to get any words out. Pastor Nicolai and I are still friends today.[9]

After Odessa, we spent a short stint in Budapest, Hungary working with the new MJBI there. Budapest is one of the most beautiful cities in the world. It is actually two cities, Buda and Pest, separated by the Danube River. While the city was tons of fun, with five spectacular bridges crossing the river, a mountain top castle and amazing restaurants at ridiculously cheap Eastern European prices, we didn't find the same spiritual openness we'd encountered in Ukraine.

One evening we took the whole Bible school to a city about two hours north of Budapest. Even though it was a small farming town, about 400 people came out to hear me. I preached a message similar to the one that overcame me and my interpreter in Ukraine. I have preached this message in Brazil, Argentina,

---

9    You can read about all our crazy exploits from being chased by wild dogs to dealing with our prostitute neighbor's ordeal with false teeth, in my book *You've Got Mail—from Odessa*. Go to our website, www.MessiahsMandate.org.

LEAVE ME ALONE—I'M JEWISH!

the US and other nations. At the conclusion of this message, 90 percent of the audience usually stands to repent of antisemitism— either for themselves or for family members. However, when I gave the invitation at this Hungarian church, *only 1 of the 400 people present stood*. I was shocked.

In this same area, just fifty years earlier, many Gentiles had turned on their Jewish neighbors, siding with the Nazis. Almost half a million Hungarian Jews, two out of every three, perished in the Holocaust and here only one person in the building felt the need to repent of antisemitism.

> The "Final Solution of the Jewish question in Hungary" got under way with a speed and efficiency surprising even the Germans: between mid April and late May, practically the entire Jewish population of the countryside was ghettoized and, in the largest deportation operation in the history of the Holocaust, between May 15 and July 9, over 437,000 people had been transported to Auschwitz-Birkenau. The speed with which the Hungarian authorities cast out Jews from society, then robbed, segregated and deported them was unprecedented in the entire history of the Holocaust.[10]

How many of those innocent victims, I wondered, were from this town in which I now stood?

I truly didn't know what to do. I wanted to start yelling at them, to do something to awaken their seared consciences, but I sensed the Lord instructing me otherwise. I had delivered my message and it was not my place to browbeat them for their lack of response. I closed the service and our stunned team returned to Budapest.

---

10      The Holocaust in Hungary, http://degob.org/index.php?showarticle=2031

It was becoming very clear that Hungary was not to be our long-term assignment. Not long after this incident, I received an invitation from Dr. Michael Brown to come and teach *Jewish Roots, Leadership* and *Evangelism* courses at the Brownsville Revival School of Ministry.

In 1995 there was a great move of God in Pensacola, Florida. Hundreds of thousands of people began to come from all over the world to visit Brownsville Assembly of God. When Elana and I heard about this revival, we wanted to visit as well. It was truly amazing—like a scene out of the book of Acts. The presence of God was so evident. After the first visit, I returned to Beth Messiah hungry to see God move similarly among us.

I was scheduled to speak that very week in our day school, *Ets Chaiyim*—Tree of Life. I showed a ten-minute video clip of the revival to the kindergarteners through eighth graders gathered. Then I asked anyone who wanted God to touch him or her like that, to come forward. About half the school came forward, the youngest ones first. I began to pray with no real expectation. I just wanted to give God an opportunity to do something special. After a minute, I concluded that nothing much was going to happen. Suddenly, I noticed the faces of several young girls, including my Sharon, begin to crinkle up and they began to cry.

It spread like fire. Within minutes nearly every student was in tears. Some were knocked down to the floor by the power of God and remained there for over an hour. Half a dozen had visions of Yeshua, and others even saw Heaven and Hell. One by one they came to the front to testify. When school ended, the kids were still strewn out all over the floor. I instructed the teachers to tell parents that we would not stop the meeting, but they could quietly come in and take their children if they needed to. I saw more than one parent carry out a limp or weeping child. When it was all over, I collected two large trash bags of tissues!

And now, I was going to have the opportunity to teach in the Bible school which was birthed out of this great revival. Actually, Dr. Brown had asked me two years earlier to come, but the Lord had given me a dream, warning me that the timing was not right.[11]

Our time in Brownsville was special. I had the privilege of teaching on *The Jewish Roots of Yeshua and the New Covenant, The History of the Church and Israel* and *God's Plan for Israel in the Last Days* to nearly 1,000 hungry young people. On more than one occasion, a weeping or devastated student would come up to me at the end of class simply to say that they were sorry, or that they never knew how bad things were for Jewish people. This was usually after teaching on The Crusades, The Inquisition or The Holocaust.

In addition we built lasting friendships. Sadly, there was a nasty split that divided the school in December of 2000. I lost many friends during that time, as there were many broken relationships and much pain. I thank the Lord that nearly all of those relationships I lost have since been restored and even strengthened.

Shortly after this split, we felt it time to move on. In the spring of 2001 the Lord spoke clearly to us: *Move back to Richmond, spend time with your parents and then move to Israel in 2003.*

Those two years in Richmond were very special. For the first, year I cut way back on ministry and worked for my father. While I don't think my presence helped his business much, it was a special time for us to be together. *Could this be the same man* who once told me that he didn't want me to work with him because he

11      If you want to read about the dream and why the Lord allowed us to go two years later, just go to www.MessiahsMandate.org and sign up for our e-mails. When you do, you will be sent my teaching, 'Messianic Jews: The Most Hated People on Earth', where I share about this experience.

*didn't want to have to look at me?* Now we were best friends. More than once I considered simply dropping out of full time ministry to be like my father and take over his business. I knew, however, I would never be fulfilled salvaging groceries—I was called to salvage souls!

In June of 2003, we jumped in a van with two friends and they drove us to Newark, New Jersey. The next day we would fly as a family to Israel. We checked into an airport hotel. From there I called my mother. On the one hand, the two years spent together with her grandkids had proven a blessing—on the other hand, it only made it that much harder on her when we left. When she answered the phone, I told her that we were all squared away in the hotel. No one responded. "Mom, are you there?"

Finally, choked up, she managed to get out a tear-filled whisper, "I can't talk... I can't stop crying..." We hung up, and I felt like the worst son in the world. Her words stung me. How could I do this to her? Of course, the next day when we landed in Israel and everyone was feeling depressed, I felt, in addition to being the worst son like I was also the worst husband and father. I had taken my family to the terror-ridden, conflict-torn Middle East! *What had I been thinking?*

The next day we woke up and everything was different. The grace of God came and we have never looked back. Living in Israel wasn't always easy for my girls, but they are all fluent in Hebrew and love the culture. While we sometimes wonder how different their growing up years would have been had we stayed in the U.S., none of them has ever said she regretted the decision to make *Aliyah*—to come home to Israel.

Those early years were special. I took two years off from most ministry to focus on Hebrew study. I would ride my bike to Hebrew school every morning and then be home in time to have lunch with Elana and the girls. We joined a congregation—Tiferet Yeshua—where only Hebrew was spoken. Most congregations offer translation into English and Russian, and sometimes Spanish. But Tiferet Yeshua had a unique vision: *reach Israelis— native-born Israelis.* Ari and Shira Sorko-Ram who founded the congregation in 1995 felt that translating to other languages drove the Israelis away because it attracted non-Hebrew speakers. Even if the language coming from the pulpit was Hebrew, the fellowship after the service would be in English if they offered translation. We were drawn to this vision.

I never dreamed that it would take me seven years to get to the place where I could preach in Hebrew, but it did. When I was finally able to, it was exhilarating. In the beginning it would take me a solid week to prepare a message. I was used to preparing messages in an hour, and now I was poring over every word, preaching the message to myself, to my daughters, to my wife and sometimes to our dog Madi (even though English is her *mother-bark!*).

When I would finally stand up to preach, I would be so nervous. I had never known this feeling before when it came to public speaking. But the Lord was breaking me of my pride. I could preach in English before 100,000 people in Africa, and here I was terrified before 100 in Israel.

Thank God, I have improved and it only takes me two days now to prepare—still much longer than in English, but I love it! I love preaching in Hebrew! I love building up the body of believers in the Holy Land. What a joy!

In 2009 I had the opportunity to go to Mubi, Nigeria, with Reinhard Bonnke and his team. One of my former students, Daniel Kolenda, was being groomed to take over the leadership of Bonnke's ministry (He now serves as president of the ministry.), which may be the largest mass evangelism ministry in the world. Daniel invited me to join them in Mubi. On that trip I saw blind eyes open and the lame walk. I saw so many miracles that after awhile it became the norm!

One young girl's story continues to stay with me. She was born blind. She was two-years-old and when Bonnke prayed for the gathered crowd of over 300,000, her mother held her blind little girl in the air. When she put her down the girl could see for the first time! When she came forward to share her story with the crowd, the little girl couldn't sit still. She just kept touching anything and everything around her. It was all new!

After the campaign, I was on my way to the airport in Yola when one of the local leaders invited me to return to hold an outreach campaign in his city. As we talked about it, the excitement grew. When we got to the airport, my plane was already on the tarmac, getting ready to head to the runway. We pulled up to a mesh fence on the side of the airport. After Pastor Mike, the one who invited me to hold a campaign, spoke persuasively to the security guard, they opened the gate. I think it also helped that Reinhard Bonnke was in the car in front of me. He is well known all over Nigeria.

I walked with my suitcases from the gate to the airplane, I never entered the airport! Now you may be thinking, *Well, that's Nigeria,* but I can assure you they have the same security protocols that we do. I never showed anyone a passport or passed through security. I paid in cash on the steps of the brand new Boeing 737. It was unreal!

Once I arrived in Lagos, their largest city, I had a whole day to seek the Lord about this idea of coming back. Suddenly I didn't have any peace about it. As I began to pray I sensed the Lord say to me, "Ron, if you come back here and preach by yourself you will bless Nigeria, but it won't touch Israel—and that is where your calling is. However, if you return here with a team of Israeli young people and let them participate, then not only will you bless Nigeria, but Israel as well. They will come back changed!"

With the help of two young Israeli leaders, we birthed the *Isaiah 2 Initiative*. Isaiah 2 speaks of a day when *the Law will go forth from Zion, the word of Lord from Jerusalem*. While I realize that, in context, it speaks of a time *after* the Lord returns to rule and reign in the millennial Kingdom, we saw a present-day application to our own lives. It wasn't enough that the remnant of Zion was being regathered to Israel. We felt we were also being called to *go out* and be *a light to the nations*.

We have since led two trips to Nigeria and one to the Ukraine. On our last trip to Nigeria, not only did we see dozens of miracles, but by the end of the week we had 67,000 decision cards from locals in attendance who had confessed faith in Yeshua! On our last night, it was amazing to witness over 100,000 Nigerians blessing the nation of Israel.

During our campaign in Gombi, two of our young men, Shlomo and Eli, were praying for a Muslim man who could not walk. He had been unable to walk for three months. They prayed for him... nothing happened... they prayed again... nothing happened... however, the third time they prayed it seemed like electricity entered him and he leapt out of his chair and began to run around rejoicing. He ran right up on the stage where those who had been healed were testifying. He took the microphone and boldly renounced Islam and embraced Yeshua.

We have so many stories like this from our trips to Africa, but I really must finish this book! You know, when I think back to the days before I embraced Yeshua, the biggest obstacle that kept me from believing was my desire for fun and excitement. What a joke!

Look at the life God has given me—living in Israel, holding mass campaigns in Africa, ministering in two dozen countries (so far), and preparing to take *The Jewish Roots of the New Covenant* message to the underground church in communist China! It's hard to even call my old life *fun* in comparison! My idea of God was so twisted and wrong. I thought serving Him would be boring, but Yeshua has given me a life, which is *anything but boring*. He promises *new life* to those who believe and, take it from me, a most unlikely candidate to herald His message, *new life* is what you'll get!

Today we are part of the leadership of *Congregation Tiferet Yeshua* in Tel Aviv. Elana teaches in a local elementary school where she is greatly loved by students and teachers alike. We are very proud of our three daughters who have grown into fine young women, two of whom have served in the Israeli Defense Forces, with the youngest just about to enlist.

As for Elana and me, we are entering a new and exciting season. This September was the first September in almost two decades that we have not sent a child off to school. We are looking forward to *dating again*. With adult children and still not fifty-years-old ourselves, we want to use this time wisely. You will recall that we were only together nine months before our wedding and then exactly nine months and three days later, our first child came along. This, therefore, is the first time in a long time that we have had the opportunity to simply be a couple.

In fact, as I pen this, it is 8:23 a.m., the time I would normally be driving the kids to their different schools, but instead I am looking out over a calm Mediterranean Sea from a beach café in Herzliya, Israel. Elana is walking on the beach and I am doing what I love most — writing. This afternoon we will worship with our congregation in Tel Aviv and then celebrate Danielle's nineteenth birthday.

As for the future: We want to continue to invest in young Israeli believers, take *The Jewish Roots of the New Testament* message all over the world, see an army of believers commit to pray for revival in Israel and continue to be a vibrant witness to the Jewish people that Yeshua is indeed, the Messiah. I can honestly say that after nearly thirty years, His fire is still burning in my soul, pushing me, driving me to make His name known in all the earth. Only through His grace and favor can we accomplish this—but He has lots of grace and favor available.

Yes, as Jews we have paid a price to believe, but only He was willing to exchange His perfect life for my awful one. I am not ashamed to say that I love Yeshua! He is my King!

May the day come when the Jewishness of *Yeshua haMashiach*, Jesus the Messiah, and the Jewishness of the New Covenant are so clear, that when presented with it, a Jewish person would say, "Are you kidding? Of course, I know Yeshua—*I'm Jewish, aren't I?!*"

# Keep up to date with what is happening in Israel!
## Plus, you can get Ron's mini-book free:

# "MESSAINIC JEWS: THE MOST HATED PEOPLE ON EARTH"

## When you sign up for our newsletter at www.MessiahsMandate.org/Updates

I want to send you my monthly newsletter free of charge so you can:

- Stay informed concerning what is happening in Israel.
- Know how to pray for Israel.
- Continue to grow in your understanding of the Jewish Roots for the faith.

When you sign up, in addition to the FREE book, you will also receive the Maoz Israel Report every month, also, free of charge! This is one of the most reputable Messianic publications coming out of Israel.

# ABOUT RON CANTOR

Messianic Jewish Communicator Ron Cantor embraced Yeshua as an 18-year-old, drug-using agnostic. He then attended CFNI in New York, and Messiah Biblical Institute, where Ron received his degree in Theology.

Ron served on the pastoral team at Beth Messiah Congregation in Rockville, Maryland, before heading overseas to Ukraine and Hungary where he and his wife Elana trained nationals for Jewish Ministry. Ron then served on the faculty of the Brownsville Revival School of Ministry teaching and mentoring young leaders.

Ron travels throughout the world from Israel sharing passionately on the Jewish Roots of the New Testament and God's broken heart for His ancient people Israel. Ron has been privileged to bring the Jewish Roots message to Brazil, Ukraine, Switzerland, France, Russia, Hungary, Israel, Germany, Argentina. Singapore, Uganda and Nigeria.

In June 2003, Ron and Elana returned with their three children to the Land of Israel where they now live and minister. During this time Ron has served as the associate leader of King of Kings Community in Jerusalem, as well as the interim senior leader.

Ron heads the Isaiah 2 Initiative, an Israeli based vision to see the good news go forth from Zion to other nations. In their trips to Nigeria and Ukraine they have seen tens of thousands of people profess faith in Yeshua.

Ron also serves with Maoz Israel blogging and making informative videos about life in Israel. He and Elana are part of the leadership team at Tiferet Yeshua, a Hebrew-speaking congregation in the heart of Tel Aviv. Ron and Elana have three daughters, Sharon, Yael and Danielle.

## YOU CAN KEEP UP WITH RON BY:

- ✡ Visiting his website at www.MessiahMandate.org
- ✡ Read his blog at www.RonCantor.com
- ✡ Becoming a Facebook friend at www.facebook.com/roncan
- ✡ Following him on Twitter at www.twitter.com/RonSCantor